The Green Agenda
A Business Guide

The Green Agenda
A Business Guide

ALAN CALDER

IT Governance Publishing

IT Governance Publishing
IT Governance Limited
Unit 3, Clive Court
Bartholomew's Walk
Cambridgeshire Business Park
Ely
Cambridgeshire
CB7 4EH
United Kingdom

www.itgovernance.co.uk

First published in the United Kingdom in 2009 by IT Governance Publishing.

ISBN 978-1-905356-98-0

FOREWORD

Climate change, global warming and, before that, the new ice age have all been fashionably topical issues about which individuals and organisations have worried themselves over the course of the last 20 years or so.

Forrester, in a late 2008 report titled *Market Overview: A Slowing Economy Won't Slow Down Corporate Green IT Initiatives*, says:

'The slowing economy will not derail efforts to make IT operations more efficient and less environmentally harmful. In fact, of responding companies that are changing the pace of their Green IT activities in response to the economic outlook, those going faster outnumber those slowing down by two to one.'

A plethora of often emotionally-held views about the reality or otherwise of climate change has emerged more recently. There is now a widely-held scientific consensus that global warming is a bad thing, will lead to the extinction of human life as we know it, and is all humanity's fault. There are also opposing arguments, although these arguments are not as well known nor as widely promulgated (perhaps because those who have them are less well funded).

Green has become an important business issue. If consumers want to buy from green organisations, then organisations have to consider their positions, their marketing strategies, their product ranges and their overall operational approach. While there is also a fast-growing market for suppliers of green products and services, there is a much larger group of organisations that do not yet know how they should respond to the green business challenge, not least because the business benefits of pursuing a green strategy are not necessarily that well articulated.

Whatever else the modern organisation does, it almost certainly had an energy dependency, and it almost certainly uses and relies on information and communications technology (ICT or, more simply, IT). Energy is an expensive commodity, and IT infrastructure and running costs in most organisations are substantial. A business cost-containment strategy that focuses on these aspects of the IT cost base is also one that has direct, quantifiable climate benefits. From a simplistic perspective, it doesn't really matter whether an organisation is motivated by a desire to save the planet or simply to save money, the results of pursuing a Green IT strategy will include both.

This guide was written to introduce, to a business audience, the opposing groups and the key climate change concepts, to provide an overview of a Green IT strategy and to set out a straightforward, bottom-line orientated Green IT action plan. The fact that this will also enable the organisation to comply[1] with the growing range of ecologically-focused regulations is an additional benefit!

---

[1] See another of the pocket guides in this series: *Compliance for Green IT*, *www.itgovernance.co.uk/products/2199*.

ABOUT THE AUTHOR

Alan Calder is a leading author on information security and IT governance issues. He is Chief Executive of IT Governance Limited, the one-stop-shop for books, tools, training and consultancy on governance, risk management and compliance. He is also Chairman of the Board of Directors of CEME, a public-private sector skills partnership.

Alan is an international authority on IT governance and, with Steve Moir, originated the innovative Calder-Moir IT Governance Framework. He is also an international expert on ISO27001 (formerly BS7799), the international security standard, about which he wrote with colleague Steve Watkins the definitive compliance guide, *IT Governance: A Manager's Guide to Data Security and BS7799/ISO17799*. This work is based on his experience of leading the world's first successful implementation of BS7799 (with the 4th edition published in May 2008) and is the basis for the UK Open University's postgraduate course on information security.

Other books written by Alan include *The Case for ISO2700; ISO27001 – Nine Steps to Success; IT Governance: Guidelines for Directors; IT Governance Today: A Practitioner's Handbook* and *IT Regulatory Compliance in the UK*.

Alan is a frequent media commentator on information security and IT governance issues, and has contributed articles and expert comment to a wide range of trade, national and online news outlets.

Alan was previously CEO of Wide Learning, a supplier of e-learning; of Focus Central London, a training and enterprise council; and of Business Link London City Partners, a government agency focused on helping growing businesses to develop. He was a member of the Information Age Competitiveness Working Group of the UK Government's Department for Trade and Industry, and was until recently a member of the DNV Certification Services Certification Committee, which certifies compliance with international standards including ISO27001.

ACKNOWLEDGEMENTS

Much of the original content of this book is drawn from the IT Governance Best Practice Report on the subject of Green IT, which was developed by our in-house research and analysis team and published towards the end of 2008. *Green IT – Reality, Benefits and Best Practices*[2] provides comprehensive, current guidance for organisations that are addressing the challenge of greening their IT operations. This pocket guide, on the other hand, is designed as an express introduction for company directors and executives to a subject that is increasingly important today to corporations the world over.

---

[2] Read about and purchase this report from *www.itgovernance.co.uk/products/1933*.

CONTENTS

Contents

INTRODUCTION

Green IT[3] will be a critical component of organisational IT strategies from 2009 onwards.

There are a range of views about what, exactly, Green IT actually is, and many of these views have a strong emotional bias. At the heart of any debate about the environmental role of IT must be an acknowledgement that the world's information and communications technologies consume a growing amount of power and have a measurably significant carbon footprint.

Such an acknowledgement does not, of course, mean that the board of directors must prioritise environmental action in any way; there is, however, a strong argument in favour of increasing one's understanding of the issues around Green IT so that one can form an intelligent and practical approach to the issue.

Some organisations are even starting to wonder what, if anything, they should do about whatever negative impact their IT operations may be having on the environment. There are, essentially, two approaches:

1   The first is that Green IT should primarily be a bottom-line focused activity that also helps to save the planet;

---

[3] Throughout this report, the term 'IT' (Information Technology) has been used rather than 'ICT' (Information and Communication Technology'). The two terms are synonymous, ICT being the preferred acronym in education and government.

2   The second is that organisations should act in the best interests of the planet, irrespective of the cost to the organisation.

Of course, the recognition that businesses are primarily interested in profitable activity may lead the observer to suspect that almost every new green business initiative nowadays is just a greenwashed decision that would have been made anyway, and that not nearly enough is being done to actually save the planet. That doesn't necessarily make it a bad decision.

What is Green IT? Why is this topic receiving such coverage and why should Green IT be of interest to a company? What are the drivers for adopting a Green IT strategy?

In our research[4], we have identified five drivers for adoption of green initiatives and, as we will show, broader green initiatives for most organisations will also have a very considerable Green IT element. Organisations pursue a green agenda for one or a combination of these five reasons:

- Saving the planet;
- Legislation/regulatory compliance;
- Improving the top line;
- Improving the bottom-line; and/or
- As part of their corporate social responsibility agenda and to promote their company reputation.

---

[4] *Green IT – Reality, Benefits and Best Practices* – an ITGP Best Practice Report, (*www.itgovernance.co.uk/products/1933*).

There is now a significant weight of scientific opinion behind the argument that changes in the world's climate are man-made and are attributable at least in part to increases in CO_2 emissions over the last 100 years. There is also a growing environmentalist culture. Environmentalism can be an emotive issue for many.

At the same time, there are a number of smaller groups who believe that the environmentalist evidence is wrong; there are others who even believe that all the climate-change arguments are merely scaremongering or that emotional feel-good environmental proposals are made simply for political gain.

However, regardless of one's individual position or the reality of the argument, there are a number of aspects of climate change – such as the outcomes of the G8 and United Nations Framework Convention on Climate Change (UNFCCC), Kyoto meetings and the growth of environmentalism – about which individual businesses can do nothing. The socio-economic-political forces that drive these developments are beyond the control of any one organisation.

There are however some facts that directly affect businesses and organisations everywhere:

- The cost of energy will increase over the medium to long term;
- Environmental regulation is increasing;
- The cultural climate is changing such that organisations and individuals are far more aware of green issues, which in turn affects purchasing decisions and company reputation; and

- The Kyoto agreement has led to the creation of an international carbon trading scheme.

These issues all affect organisations and, unless the organisation responds appropriately, they can also have a negative impact on corporate profitability.

The increasing cost of energy

There is widespread evidence that the long-term cost of energy is rising[5]. The US Energy Information Administration[6] (EIA) report suggests that factors such as the continued increase in demand for oil (particularly in countries such as China and India) and concerns about the diminishing supply have all contributed to this price increase[7]. *The Economist*[8] also points to supply concerns caused by the war in Iraq, conflict in Venezuela and a diminution of supply in Russia, and the OPEC cartel's control over oil prices.

The short-term oil price reduction linked to the 2008-10 economic recession does not change the long-term prognostication for energy prices.

---

[5] 'Rising Demand for Oil Provokes New Energy Crisis', Jad Mouawad, 9 November 2007, *www.nytimes.com/2007/11/09/business/worldbusiness/09oil.html?_r=2&oref=slogin&oref=slogin*.
[6] *www.eia.doe.gov*.
[7] 'Annual Energy Outlook 2008', June 2008, *www.eia.doe.gov/oiaf/aeo/pdf/0383(2008).pdf*.
[8] 'Oil in troubled waters', *The Economist*, 28 April 2005, *www.economist.com/surveys/displaystory.cfm?story_id=E1_PRROGNP*.

Increasing environmental regulation

Climate-related regulation is also on the increase. Organisations need to have an awareness and understanding of the relevant regulations and legislation so that they can ensure that they take appropriate compliance action[9].

The green culture affects purchasing decisions and company reputation

Those organisations that, for any one of the five reasons identified earlier, are committed to a green action plan, tend to want to purchase from companies who themselves manufacture using green materials and processes, rather from those who do not.

The current corporate and governance climate is also one in which companies are increasingly encouraged to consider their reputation and their corporate social responsibility (CSR) or social responsibility strategy. Michael Peeters[10] says that *'the private sector is coming under increasing pressure from customers, shareholders and investors in terms of how they deal with environmental issues'*.

Carbon trading and carbon caps

Carbon trading and carbon cap-and-trade schemes are used in a voluntary or mandatory capacity to reduce CO_2 emissions and offset the impact of the

---

[9] See *Compliance for Green IT*, *www.itgovernance.co.uk/products/2199*.
[10] 'Waste not, want not', Michael Peeters and Helen Keele, *Green Computing*, 24 July 2008.

environmental damage caused elsewhere. These schemes are still very much in their infancy and have had varying degrees of success. The evidence from the increasing amount and scope of the European and US state legislation is that this will remain an issue for some organisations at least for the next few years.

Implications for IT

The steady, long-term impact of rising energy costs pushes organisations to reduce their energy consumption. Those organisations that have high energy costs must take more urgent action; this is particularly important for those organisations with significant IT investments, where the consequences of decisions made today will play themselves out over many years. For example, Brill reported in 2007 that:

'The three year cost of powering and cooling servers is currently 1.5 times the cost of purchasing server hardware. Future projections extending out to 2012 show this multiplier increasing to 22 times the cost of the hardware under worst case assumptions and to almost three times under even the best-case assumptions' [11].

According to Gartner[12], ICT has been blamed for creating two per cent of the world's total CO_2 emissions, which is equivalent to that due to

---

[11] 'Data Center Energy Efficiency and Productivity', Kenneth Brill, 2007, The Uptime Institute, *http://uptimeinstitute.org/component/option,com_frontpage/Itemid,1/*.
[12] 'Managing the company's carbon footprint', Economist Intelligence Unit, *The Economist*, 2008.

airlines – and this statistic has been widely quoted. In addition, Smart2020[13] report that *'the carbon generated from materials and manufacture is about one quarter of the overall ICT carbon footprint, the rest coming from its use'*.

A key operational focus of IT has traditionally been to ensure reliability and to minimise outages; energy consumption has usually only been of secondary importance. In addition, as IT technology has moved forward, the power and storage capacity of computers has constantly increased while chips have become denser. Processing and storage requirements for computers have increased. All this has led to an exponential increase in the IT industry's energy consumption over the past 20 years.

One result of the Green Agenda has been a drive to increase the energy-efficiency of IT equipment, to recycle resources and dispose of IT equipment in an environmentally sensitive way. This not only protects the environment but also reduces energy costs. At the same time, organisations are increasingly conscious that public environmental awareness can affect their reputation and brand image. Manufacturers whose products meet recognised green criteria may have a competitive edge in the market place.

This pocket guide gives a calm and balanced overview of all the issues that organisations have to consider, and provides:

---

[13] 'Smart2020: Enabling the low carbon economy in the information age', The Climate Group, Global e-sustainability initiative (GeSI), www.smart2020.org.

1   A brief summary of both sides of the Green IT debate;
2   A discussion of the corporate social responsibility issues;
3   A workable description of the core Green IT definitions and what they mean within a business environment (complete with a glossary of Green IT terms and, at different points through the report, explanations of some of the key metrics used in this area);
4   A description of best practice for implementing a Green IT action plan.

CHAPTER 1: THE GREEN AGENDA

Proponents of what we have called the Green Agenda argue that the world is in the grips of either global warming and/or climate destabilisation and/or climate change. These changes are said to be anthropogenic, or caused by human-induced CO_2 emissions. Furthermore, it is argued, these changes may ultimately be destructive of human society and could threaten the very survival of humanity. Urgent steps are required to counter this effect, which may of necessity be both expensive and inconvenient.

At the heart of the Green Agenda is the fact that humanity uses fuels which are largely oil-based or coal-based, which are non-renewable and whose use, it is said, is non-sustainable. These fuels are carbon based and release CO_2 (and other gases) when used. The CO_2 emissions from carbon-based fuels cause the greenhouse effect. It is claimed that a runaway greenhouse effect could have catastrophic consequences on the world and that this would include increased drought, flooding and hurricanes, as well as economic and social disruption and, ultimately, the collapse of society as we know it. Some of the most notable and influential presentations of the argument that climate change is human-caused include:

- The reports of the Intergovernmental Panel on Climate Change (IPCC);
- The United Nations Framework Convention on Climate Change (UNFCCC) and the Kyoto Protocol;

- The Stern Report;
- The film 'An Inconvenient Truth' presented by former United States Vice President Al Gore;
- The Gaia hypothesis formulated by James Lovelock.

Energy and carbon footprint

There are a handful of concepts whose understanding is critical to the whole green debate and to the effectiveness of any Green IT strategy. Energy usage, CO_2 (and greenhouse gases) and carbon footprint are at the heart of any attempt to respond to the Green Agenda.

Energy is the resource which enables us to live and in technical terms, to do work. Ultimately all energy comes from the sun. There are many forms of energy including heat energy which is measured in temperature and electrical energy. Energy can be transformed but it can't be created. For example, coal is used to generate electrical energy which in turn is used for heat and light. Fuel is a store of energy.

Energy is categorised into that which is sustainable or non-sustainable, and renewable or non-renewable. The words sustainable and renewable are sometimes used synonymously, but they have slightly different meanings.

Wikipedia defines sustainable energy as energy sources which 'meet the needs of the present without compromising the ability of future generations to meet their needs'.

Renewable energy is that which is naturally replenished. For example, energy derived from the wind and the sun is naturally replenished, whereas oil and coal reserves are absolutely limited. Hydroelectric power is an example of renewable energy sourced from coastal tides, waves or fast flowing rivers. Other examples of renewable energy include wind power and solar power. The Earth also produces biomass, which is renewable energy in the form of crops, wood and waste from animals and algae. Geothermal energy comes from heat stored underground.

Fossil fuels such as oil, gas, or coal are a non-renewable energy source derived from the organic remains of past life. Fossil fuels consist primarily of hydrocarbons.

According to the *Rough Guide to Energy*, around four-fifths (67%) of the global energy we use today comes from fossil fuels.

Different energy sources are used in different sectors. Motorised transport is fuelled almost entirely by oil, while heating is fuelled by a mixture of gas, oil, wood, coal and other energy sources.

Energy sources and consumption vary a great deal by country. For example, China uses its own reserves of coal. Japan relies on nuclear power plus imported oil and liquefied natural gas. Canada uses hydroelectricity from its rivers and mountains, which is obviously not an option for countries such as the Netherlands. 30% of the global population does not have access to electricity.

Demand for energy has almost doubled in the last three decades, due to the rise in the global population and the increased energy demands in developing countries including Brazil, Russia, India and China (known as the BRIC countries).

Burning fossil fuels is said to be a major contributor to climate change. When fossil fuels are burnt, they release CO_2 and other gases, which are known in this debate as the greenhouse gases (often referred to in the green press as GHG).

Carbon footprint is the measurement of all the greenhouse gases produced by individuals and/or groups. It relates to the amount of greenhouse gases produced daily and yearly through burning fossil fuels for electricity, heating and transportation, etc. So, for example, driving an average sized car about 12,000 miles a year will generate 3.5 tonnes of CO_2 in that year.

A carbon footprint is measured in units of tonnes (or kg) of carbon dioxide equivalent[14].

There is a level of sophistication to this definition; a carbon footprint is said to be made up of a primary and secondary footprint. The primary footprint is a measure of emissions of CO_2 from the burning of fossil fuels in energy consumption and transportation. The secondary footprint is a measure of CO_2 emissions from the lifecycle of products and equipment which we use.

Fossil fuels are not renewable, and our fossil fuel resources may (or may not) be running down. The Peak Oil theory refers to the point at which half of the world's accessible reserves will have been

---

[14] 'What Is A Carbon Footprint?'
www.carbonfootprint.com/carbonfootprint.html.

extracted. The International Energy Agency in their World Energy Outlook for 2004 estimated oil production to peak at some point between 2013 and 2037, and this prediction has been widely quoted. However, the complication to this is that reserves of oil used in this equation are only counted commercially if they can be extracted at a profit. This tends to mean that, the higher the price of oil, the more oil is available.

Oil companies prefer to argue that the technologies for extracting oil are improving, as a result of which the commercially available reserves of oil are increasing. The US Geological Survey estimates that there is much more oil in the ground than has so far been discovered. However, most of the data on oil supplies is held by OPEC, which the *Rough Guide to Energy* says 'keeps a tight lid on its numbers and methods'.

Electrical energy is usually measured in joules. Power, which is defined as energy used in a certain amount of time, is measured in watts. A watt is a unit of power equal to one joule per second.

According to Wikipedia, nuclear energy has the potential to be sustainable. It also produces little CO_2. France is a significant user of nuclear power and the nuclear energy generated in its power stations provides 80% of its current energy needs[15]. Many people, though, are against nuclear power and memories of events like the Three Mile Island accident and the Chernobyl disaster form powerful strands in their resistance.

---

[15] *www.npr.org/templates/story/story.php?storyId=5369 610.*

The IPCC

The IPCC (the Intergovernmental Panel on Climate Change) is a scientific intergovernmental body set up by the World Meteorological Organisation (WMO) and the United Nations Environment Programme (UNEP) in 1988.

The IPCC was established to:

'Provide the decision makers and others interested in climate change with an objective source of information about climate change. Its role is to assess on a comprehensive, objective, open and transparent basis the latest scientific, technical and socio-economic literature produced worldwide relevant to the understanding of the risk of human-induced climate change, its observed and projected impacts and options for adaptation and mitigation'[16].

The latest assessment report from the IPCC, Climate Change 2007: Synthesis report[17], states that:

'Warming of the climate system is unequivocal, as is now evident from observations of increases in global average air and ocean temperatures, widespread melting of snow and ice and rising global average sea level..........
Many natural systems, on all continents and in some oceans, are being affected by regional climate changes..........

---

[16] Intergovernmental Panel on Climate Change, *www.ipcc.ch/about/index.htm*.
[17] 'Climate Change 2007: Synthesis report', adopted at IPCC, Spain, 12-17 November 2007, *www.ipcc.ch/pdf/assessment-report/ar4/syr/ar4_syr.pdf*.

Global annual <u>anthropogenic</u> greenhouse gas emissions have grown by 70% between 1970 and 2004..........................
It is likely that there is a discernible human-induced warming averaged over each continent (except Antarctica).........'

However, the IPCC also states that:

'Climate data coverage remains limited in some regions and there is a notable lack of geographic balance in data and literature on observed changes in natural and managed systems, with marked scarcity in developing countries.........

Difficulties remain in reliably simulating and attributing observed temperature changes to natural or human causes at smaller than continental scales.'

The reports and analysis from the IPCC are the most significant and respected component of the whole Green Agenda; the scientific consensus that underpins this work is clearly substantial.

The Kyoto Protocol

The United Nations Framework Convention on Climate Change (UNFCCC) entered into force on 21 March 1994[18]. 192 countries are formal members of the UNFCCC. The UNFCCC was set up in order to:

---

[18] 'The United Nations Framework Convention on Climate Change', *http://unfccc.int/essential_background/convention/items/2627.php*.

- Gather and share information on GHG emissions, national policies and best practices.
- Launch national strategies for addressing GHGs and adapting to expected impacts, including the provision of financial and technological support to developing countries.
- Co-operate in preparing for adaptation to the impacts of climate change.

The UNFCCC negotiated the Kyoto Protocol, which was intended to be more powerful and legally binding than the UNFCCC. The Kyoto Protocol is a *'legally binding agreement between signed-up countries to meet emissions reduction targets of 5.4% relative to 1990 levels by 2012'*[19]. It is not clear that the proposed emissions reduction will have a significant positive impact on climate change.

34 countries signed up to this protocol, which was negotiated in December 1997 in Kyoto, Japan, and came into force in February 2005. The Kyoto agreement is often quoted in combination with the Stern Report (see below) to represent landmarks in international awareness in reducing expected climate change.

The emissions reduction targets refer to those gases which cause the greenhouse effect.

Estimating the levels of greenhouse gas emissions and removals is therefore part of the Kyoto agreement. The Kyoto greenhouse gases[20] are:

---

[19] Kyoto agreement, key points, *www.climate-concern.com/Kyoto%20Agreement.htm*.
[20] Often referred to in the green literature as GHG.

1   Carbon dioxide (CO_2)
2   Methane (CH_4)
3   Nitrous oxide (N_2O)
4   Hydrofluorocarbons (HFCs)
5   Perfluorocarbons (PFCs)
6   Sulphur hexafluoride (SF_6).

These are the six main greenhouse gases covered by the targets set out in the Kyoto Protocol. Wikipedia describes the GHGs as 'those gaseous constituents of the atmosphere, both natural and anthropogenic, that absorb and emit radiation at specific wavelengths within the spectrum of thermal infrared radiation emitted by the Earth's surface, the atmosphere itself, and by clouds'[21].

The Kyoto agreement was not ratified by the Bush presidency in the US, Australia, China, India or Russia, and discussions for a post-2012 agreement are currently underway.

The main significance of the Kyoto agreement is that it sets emission targets for countries which have signed up to it. As a consequence of Kyoto, participating countries have agreed set limits to national CO_2 emissions, which have led to the development of carbon trading between Kyoto members.

In early December 2007 the UN held a meeting to agree the Framework Convention on Climate Change in Bali[22]. Whilst this meeting was not

---

[21] 'Greenhouse gas', Wikipedia,
http://en.wikipedia.org/wiki/Greenhouse_gas.
[22] 'United Nations Framework Convention on Climate Change', The road to Copenhagen 2009,
http://unfccc.int/2860.php.

without controversy (as with the preceding Kyoto meeting in 1997), this meeting of the international scientific and policy making community again pushed the issue of global warming higher up the international agenda.

The Stern Review

The Stern Review[23] was commissioned by the UK government and published in October 2006. It was led by Lord Stern, the then Head of the Government Economic Service and former World Bank Chief Economist. The review predicts a likely rise of between 2–5°C in global mean temperatures between 2030 and 2060. The report warns that this warming will have many severe impacts. For example:

- Melting glaciers will increase flood risk and then water supplies, threatening the Indian sub-continent, parts of China and the Andes in South America.
- In Africa, the increased temperatures will 'seriously affect' crop yields.
- There will be 'serious risks' of flooding in Bangladesh, Vietnam, the small islands in the Caribbean and the Pacific and large coastal cities such as Tokyo, New York, Cairo and London.

The Stern Review attributes the causes of global warming to human activities, concluding that

---

[23] 'Stern Review on the economics of climate change', HM Treasury, UK, 2005, *www.occ.gov.uk/activities/stern.htm*.

'there is no other plausible explanation for the observed warming for at least the past 50 years'.

An Inconvenient Truth

The film 'An Inconvenient Truth' is a documentary about global warming, created and presented by former United States Vice President Al Gore. The film premiered at the 2006 Sundance Film Festival and was released by Paramount in November 2006. The film is designed to persuasively present four main hypotheses[24]:

1   Global average temperatures have been rising significantly over the past half century and are likely to continue doing so;
2   Climate change is mainly attributable to man-made emissions of carbon dioxide, methane and nitrous oxide;
3   Climate change will, if unchecked, have significant adverse effects on the world and its populations;
4   There are measures which individuals and governments can take which will help to reduce climate change or mitigate its effects.

The DVD version of the film is accompanied by a study guide[25] for schools which can be

---

[24] England and Wales High Court (Administrative Court) Decisions, before Mr Justice Burton, between Stuart Dimmock, Claimant, and Secretary of State for Education and Skills, (now Secretary of State for Children, Schools and Families), *www.bailii.org/ew/cases/EWHC/Admin/2007/2288.html*.
[25] *http://prod.takepart.com/social_network/action/ait/stu dyguides.html*.

downloaded. This contains a series of lessons designed for science classrooms.

Al Gore and the IPCC were jointly awarded the Nobel Peace Prize in October 2007 'for their efforts to build up and disseminate greater knowledge about man-made climate change and to lay the foundations for the measures that are needed to counteract such change'[26].

In the UK, the film is being shown to all children. In the US, the producer of the film offered 50,000 free DVDs to the National Science Teachers Association (NSTA) for distribution to schools. The NSTA felt unable to take this offer up because their policies prohibit them from endorsing any product. However, they did offer to provide a link to the film on NSTA's website and announced the free availability of the DVD to science teachers.

The film was apparently banned in Seattle in the US, because it was 'too controversial'[27].

In the UK, it was decided by the then Secretary of State for Education and Skills in 2007 to distribute the film to every state secondary school in the United Kingdom as part of a pack containing four other short films and a cross-reference to an educational website (Teachernet) containing a guidance note. This was challenged in the High Court by one parent, who argued that the distribution of the film in schools was unlawful.

---

[26] The Nobel Peace Prize 2007, 12 October 2007, *http://nobelprize.org/nobel_prizes/peace/laureates/2007/press.html*.
[27] 'Scottish schools to show climate change film', *The Guardian*, 18 January 2007, *www.guardian.co.uk/education/2007/jan/18/schools.uk2*.

The findings of the subsequent court case were that the views of the film are political and alarmist and that the film contains scientific errors[28]. The scientific errors included:

1   Al Gore claiming that there was an exact fit between a graph showing the rise in CO_2 in the atmosphere and the rise in temperature, which is not the case.
2   The cause of Hurricane Katrina of 2005 was ascribed to global warming. However, there is insufficient evidence to support this.
3   Mr Gore says that polar bears have drowned by having to swim long distances to find ice. However, this is not the case.

The Court's ruling was that the film, which in any event had already been distributed to schools, should not be banned. However, the guidance notes were to be changed to say:

'[Schools] must bear in mind the following points:

- *AIT promotes partisan political views (that is to say, one sided views about political issues);*
- *Teaching staff must be careful to ensure that they do not themselves promote those views;*
- *In order to make sure of that, they should take care to help pupils examine the scientific evidence critically (rather than simply accepting what is said at face value) and to*

---

[28] England and Wales High Court (Administrative Court) Decisions, before Mr Justice Burton, between Stuart Dimmock, Claimant, and Secretary of State for Education and Skills (now Secretary of State for Children, Schools and Families), *www.bailii.org/ew/cases/EWHC/Admin/2007/2288.html*.

> *point out where Gore's view may be*
> *inaccurate or departs from that of mainstream*
> *opinion;*

- *Where the film suggests that views should take*
  particular action at the political level (e.g. to
  lobby their democratic representatives to vote
  for measures to cut carbon emissions),
  teaching staff must be careful to offer pupils a
  balanced presentation of opposing views and
  not to promote either the view expressed in the
  film or any other particular view.'

The Gaia hypothesis

The Gaia hypothesis was first formulated by James Lovelock in the 1960s. The hypothesis is that the Earth is a self-regulating living being. This co-ordinated system of living organisms maintains the climatic and biogeochemical conditions on Earth in a preferred homeostasis. James Lovelock says that *'The evolution of organisms and their material environment proceeds as a single tightly coupled process from which self-regulation of the environment, at a habitable state, appears as an emergent phenomenon'*[29].

Lovelock argues that this Gaia balance has been upset by humanity's CO_2 emissions and predicts serious environmental challenges. He uses the analogy of a failing kidney which requires dialysis to regulate the body's blood sugar levels. The difficulty with this is that artificial, technological fixes are typically not as reliable as the natural

---

[29] 'Gaia Theory', Channel 4 Nature, *www.channel4.com/science/microsites/S/science/nature/ gaia.html*.

ones. Lovelock feels that, in a similar fashion, *'mankind is taking over the reins of global geochemical balance. Industrial production of fixed nitrogen for fertilizer now matches the natural rate of nitrogen fixation on the planet. Rates of fossil-fuel CO_2 emission dwarf the natural rate of CO_2 release in volcanic gases*[30]. Lovelock's conclusion, by analogy, is that the biosphere of the Earth will soon be beset by all manner of unanticipated complications.

James Lovelock, although formerly opposed to nuclear power, now argues that nuclear power is the key to dealing with global warming and that fears about nuclear power have been exaggerated. He now argues, with others, that *'nuclear power is at least as environmentally friendly as traditional sources of renewable energy, making it part of the solution to global warming and the world's growing need for energy. Nuclear power plants produce little carbon dioxide emissions and the radioactive waste produced is minimal and well-contained, especially compared to fossil fuels*[31].

The G8 versus the G5

The G8 group comprises leaders from eight countries which are Canada, France, Germany, Italy, Japan, Russia, United Kingdom and United States. The G8 represent the most industrialised and developed countries. The leaders have a face-

---

[30] 'James Lovelock's Gloomy Vision', RealClimate, 13 February 2006, *www.realclimate.org/index.php?p=256*.
[31] 'Sustainable energy', Wikipedia, *http://en.wikipedia.org/wiki/Sustainable_energy#Nuclear_power*.

to-face meeting each year, the aim of which is to 'tackle global challenges through discussion and action'[32]. The group was formed subsequent to the oil crisis of the early 1970s.

In July 2008, the G8 leaders met in Toyako on the Japanese island of Hokkaido. Following this meeting, the Japanese Prime Minister, Yasuo Fukuda, said: *'after today's G8 summit we agreed to set the aim for a reduction of the entire global emissions of gases to 50% by 2050 as a target to be taken up by the entire world. This strengthened the pledge made at the G8 summit in 2007 to "seriously consider" the cuts*[33].

The G5 group, in contrast, comprises leaders from the five fastest developing countries: China, India, Brazil, Mexico and South Africa. In July 2008, the G5 met on the day before the G8 meeting. The section on climate change in the G5 declaration said that *'a shared vision including a long-term global goal for emissions reduction must be based on an equitable burden-sharing paradigm that ensures equal sustainable development potential for all citizens of the world and takes into account historical responsibility and respective capabilities as a fair and just approach*[34].

---

[32] Profile: G8, BBC News, *http://news.bbc.co.uk/2/hi/americas/country_profiles/3777557.stm*.

[33] 'A deal on climate change – but then the backlash', *The Guardian*, 9 July 2008, *www.guardian.co.uk/environment/2008/jul/09/3*.

[34] 'Climate: G8 and G5 leaders issue different climate messages', Third World Network, 11 July 2008, *www.twnside.org.sg/title2/climate/info.service/climate.change.20080702.htm*.

There is, behind the carefully selected words, a clear divergence: the G8 want the entire world to contribute to saving the planet, whereas the G5 want G8 countries to make a significant contribution, one that doesn't interfere with the right of the G5 countries to continue their own industrialisation.

26

CHAPTER 2: A HISTORY OF ENVIRONMENTALISM

The history of environmentalism stretches back some 300 years, and it is useful to be able to place today's approach in its historic context:

1703 to 1850	The Industrial Revolution caused a previously unprecedented amount of forest clearance and land drainage.
1850	Nature writers were talking about a respect for nature.
1892	John Muir founded the US conservation organisation to encourage the US government to protect parts of the environment. He was opposed by politicians and companies such as timber companies. At about the same time, national parks were declared in Australia, New Zealand and Canada.
1893	The RSPB (Royal Society for the Protection of Birds) was established in the UK.
1894	The National Trust was established in the UK.
1900 to 1950s	There was a growing awareness of environmental issues such as endangered wildlife and a sense of a

responsibility to nature.

1960s	The Gaia hypothesis was first formulated by James Lovelock.

1962	Rachel Carson's book *Silent Spring* was published. It dramatised the effects of chemicals contaminating the environment and thereby humans. In the book, the insecticide DDT enters the food chain and results in a high risk of cancer.

1971	The groups Friends of the Earth and Greenpeace were established.

1972	The United Nations Conference on the Human Environment met, attended by 113 nations concerned about issues such as acid rain and the industrial poisoning of seas. The summit exposed a rift between the developed and the developing world. The issue was the developed world's exploitation of natural resources in a way that not only degraded the environment, but also perpetuated the unequal distribution of wealth. This social divide remains in place today and has arguably widened.

Mid	Fears about the ozone layer were mooted. It was claimed[35] that some

---

[35] *http://science.nasa.gov/headlines/y2006/images/ozone/20questions.pdf*.

1970s	human-produced chemicals, notably CFCs (which were found in aerosol cans and air conditioners) could destroy ozone and deplete the ozone layer which exists around the earth. CFCs are chlorine, fluorine and carbon gases which are known collectively as chlorofluorocarbons. This is expected to increase the incidence of skin cancer and eye cataracts. The most severe impact of CFCs was the depletion in the ozone layer, particularly over Antarctica, and this became known as the Ozone hole.
1975	The first G8 meeting was held at the economic summit convened by the President of France and attended by leaders from Germany, Japan, the UK, and the US[36].
1975 to 1976	Claims about global cooling were made for the first time. In 1975 *Newsweek* wrote of 'ominous signs' that temperatures were dipping[37]. In 1976 the *National Geographic* quoted the US National Science Board as reporting that 'judging from the record of the past interglacial ages, the present time of high

---

[36] 'Meeting of G8 Justice and Home Affairs Ministers', *www.usdoj.gov/criminal/cybercrime/g82004/g8_backgro und.html*.

[37] *http://discovermagazine.com/2006/feb/global-cooling*.

temperatures should be drawing to an end... leading into the next glacial age ...'.[38]

1983	The UN General Assembly created the UN World Commission on Environment and Development. It appointed Dr Gro Harlem Brundtland, the first woman Prime Minister of Norway, as chairperson. Four years later, she published the Brundtland Report, and coined the term sustainable development. The report combined environmental and economic considerations, and defined sustainability as: 'development that meets the needs of the present without compromising the ability of future generations to meet their own needs'.
1987	The Montreal Protocol on Substances that Deplete the Ozone Layer was signed by 20 nations. This established controls on the production and consumption of halogen source gases known to cause ozone depletion. There is now widespread opinion that the ozone layer is recovering and should be restored between 2030 and 2070. NASA argues that about half of the recent trend is due to CFC

---

[38] *http://findarticles.com/p/articles/mi_m0JZS/is_21_20/ai_n25098218.*

reductions[39]. However, in addition to CFCs, sunspots, the weather, changing wind patterns and volcanoes contribute to holes in the ozone layer. In addition, there may be other sources of natural or man-made variability which affect the ozone layer.

The Montreal Protocol created a precedent for international agreements to reduce gas emissions, and is quoted in the Kyoto Protocol[40]. It is viewed by environmentalists as an example and proof that such gas emission reduction initiatives can reverse the trend of human caused damage to the environment.

1988   The Intergovernmental Panel on Climate Change (IPCC) was established by the World Meteorological Organisation (WMO) and the United Nations Environment Programme (UNEP). It was made up of governments, scientists and the United Nations body. The aim of the IPCC was and is to establish an objective source of information on

---

[39] *http://science.nasa.gov/headlines/y2006/26may_ozone.htm*.

[40] 'Annex A, Kyoto Protocol to the United Nations Framework convention on climate change', United Nations 1998, *http://unfccc.int/resource/docs/convkp/kpeng.pdf#page=20*.

climate change.

1990s   The lack of landfill space in which to bury our rubbish and a need to conserve resources became an issue which meant that recycling bins began to appear. Simultaneously, green products grew in number and range on the supermarket shelves.

1992   The Earth Summit took place in Rio, Brazil. It emphasised how the planet's environmental problems are linked to the economy and to social justice issues. The attending world leaders agreed to combat global warming, protect biodiversity and stop using dangerous poisons. Global warming became the major issue. Carbon dioxide gas, released from burning fossil fuels like petrol, coal, oil and gas, was causing the planet to heat up. The resulting melting ice caps and rising sea levels threatened the whole world. The Kyoto Protocol, introduced at Rio, required signatories to cut carbon dioxide emissions by five per cent between 2008 and 2012. Many nations signed up to it, but some developed countries such as the US did not.

1994   The United Nations Framework Convention on Climate Change (UNFCCC) entered into force.

2005   The Kyoto Protocol came into force. This was a legally binding agreement signed up to by 34 countries to reduce GHG emissions by 2012.

2006   The Stern Review assessing the nature of the economic challenges of climate change and how they can be met was published.

2006   The film 'An Inconvenient Truth' was premiered at the 2006 Sundance Film Festival.

2007   The 4th Assessment Reports of the IPCC concluded that warming of the climate system was unequivocal, and that this warming was affecting many natural systems and that it is *likely* that this is human-induced.

CHAPTER 3: ECO-DISASTER: THE SCEPTICS

While the Green Agenda dominates Western environmental debate, has a high public profile and claims to represent the settled, consensus view of the worldwide scientific community, there are a number of counter-arguments which suggest that the consensus is not as consensual as is usually represented. These counter-arguments are expressed in, or by:

- The sunspot theory;
- *The Skeptical Environmentalist*;
- The UK television Channel 4 programme, 'The Great Global Warming Swindle';
- The work of the Danish National Space Center;
- The opposition of the developing world;
- Accusations of alarmism;
- Identification of inconsistent record keeping;
- Special pleading.

The sunspot theory

A sunspot is defined by Wikipedia[41] as *'a region that has a lower temperature than its surroundings and has intense magnetic activity, which inhibits convection, forming areas of reduced surface temperature'*. The sunspot theory is that climate

---

[41] 'Sunspot', Wikipedia, *http://en.wikipedia.org/wiki/Sunspot*.

change is caused by changes in the sun's activity[42], not by increases in CO_2 emissions. Sunspots come and go in an approximate 11-year cycle. When there are fewer sunspots, the climate is colder, when there are more, the climate is warmer.

Proponents of the sunspot theory as a cause of global warming say that *'over the past few hundred years, there has been a steady increase in the numbers of sunspots, a trend that has accelerated in the past century, just at the time when the Earth has been getting warmer'*[43].

However, critics argue that *'although sunspots alter the amount of energy the Earth gets from the sun, this is not enough to impact global climate change'*[44]. However, they do say that *'more complicated solar mechanisms could possibly be driving climate change in ways we don't yet understand'*. Sami Solanki of the Max Planck Institute for Solar System Research in Lindau, Germany is quoted as saying that *'there are numerous studies that find a correlation [between solar variation and Earth climate]......There may be other mechanisms acting for the way that the sun influences climate'*.

---

[42] 'The Great Global Warming Swindle, The Arguments',
www.channel4.com/science/microsites/G/great_global_warming_swindle/arguments_6.html.
[43] 'Sunspots reaching 1,000 year high', Dr David Whitehouse, BBC News,
http://news.bbc.co.uk/2/hi/science/nature/3869753.stm.
[44] 'Don't Blame Sun for Global Warming, Study Says', National Geographic News, 13 September 2006,
http://news.nationalgeographic.com/news/2006/09/0609 13-sunspots.html.

The Skeptical Environmentalist

The Skeptical Environmentalist is a still controversial book, written by Danish author, academic and environmentalist Bjørn Lomborg, and first published in 1998. Bjørn Lomborg is director of the Copenhagen Consensus Center. In this book, Lomborg argues that many claims such as declining energy resources and some aspects of global warming are unsupported by analysis of the relevant data. Lomborg challenges beliefs that the environmental situation is getting worse. He criticises the way in which he feels that many environmental organisations make selective and misleading use of the scientific evidence[45]. Lomborg and his book were both subjected to widespread denigration by those who support the scientific consensus. Lomborg has subsequently written *Cool It*[46], which was published in 2007. In this book he argues that:

'Any of the elaborate and expensive actions now being considered to stop global warming will cost hundreds of billions of dollars, are often based on emotional rather than strictly scientific assumptions, and may very well have little impact on the world's temperature for hundreds of years. Rather than starting with the most radical procedures, we should first focus our resources on more immediate concerns, such as fighting malaria and HIV/AIDS and assuring and maintaining a safe, fresh water supply – which can

---

[45] Cambridge University Press Catalogue, *The Skeptical Environmentalist, Measuring the Real State of the World*, *www.itgovernance.co.uk/products/1881*.
[46] *www.itgovernance.co.uk/products/1880*.

be addressed at a fraction of the cost and save millions of lives within our lifetime.'

He asks why the debate over climate change has stifled rational dialogue and killed meaningful dissent[47]. Lomborg also argues that global warming would be 'rather slight' and that even if warming is real, then it is unavoidable 'barring massive and devastating deindustrialisation'[48]. Lomborg describes Kyoto as 'Institutionalised hypocrisy'[49] and also asserts that:

'The unwavering certainty that CO_2 cuts are the best way to help is problematic………For many writers and world leaders, global warming has been seized upon as a subject that can lift them out of the tedious bickering of distributional politics and instead allow them to position themselves as humanitarians………… It actually makes some taxes popular, and yet the true costs of policies are far removed. At a recent climate demonstration in London, protesters actually chanted: "What do we want? Carbon taxes! When do we want them? Now!"………… when the time comes to commit to the political rhetoric of global warming, support suddenly withers away, because governments know that CO_2 cuts will quickly become very expensive and are likely be politically dangerous.'

---

[47] *www.itgovernance.co.uk/products/1880.*
[48] *The Politically Incorrect Guide to Global Warming and Environmentalism,* Christopher Horner, 2007.
[49] Bjørn Lomborg: Kyoto's cult of 'Institutionalised hypocrisy', *National Post,* 2 November 2007, *http://network.nationalpost.com/np/blogs/fullcomment/ar chive/2007/11/02/bjorn-lomborg-kyoto-s-cult-of-institutionalized-hypocrisy.aspx.*

The Great Global Warming Swindle

The UK Channel 4 programme, 'The Great Global Warming Swindle'[50], was aired on UK television in March 2007. This programme agrees that climate change is a reality and that the earth is warming. However, it disputes whether this is caused by human action or by CO_2 emissions. The programme says that CO_2 is produced in far larger quantities by many natural means, and that human emissions are miniscule in comparison. Volcanic emissions and carbon dioxide from animals, bacteria, decaying vegetation and the ocean outweigh human production several times over.

The programme also argued that the effect of cosmic radiation and solar activity may explain fluctuations in global temperatures more precisely than the carbon dioxide theory. This is also known as the Sunspot theory, which we discussed earlier.

In addition, the film makers argue that the present single-minded focus on reducing carbon emissions may have the unintended consequence of stifling development in the Third World, prolonging endemic poverty and disease. Channel 4 says that:

'Research presented in the film showed that the effect of cosmic radiation, and solar activity may explain fluctuations in global temperatures more precisely than the carbon dioxide theory. Solar activity, over the last several hundred years, correlates, on a decadal basis, with temperature. There is some evidence to suggest that the rise in

---

[50] 'The Great Global Warming Swindle', Channel 4, *www.channel4.com/science/microsites/G/great_global_warming_swindle/programme.html*.

carbon dioxide lags behind the temperature rise by 800 years and therefore can't be the cause of it. If greenhouse warming were happening, then scientists predict that the troposphere (the layer of the earth's atmosphere roughly 10-15km above us) should heat up faster than the surface of the planet, but data collected from satellites and weather balloons doesn't seem to support this. CO_2 is produced in far larger quantities by many natural means: human emissions are miniscule in comparison. Volcanic emissions and carbon dioxide from animals, bacteria, decaying vegetation and the ocean outweigh our own production several times over. Solar activity very precisely matches the plot of temperature change over the last 100 years. It correlates well with the anomalous post-war temperature dip, when global carbon dioxide levels were rising.'

They argue that it is not economically viable to ask people in developing countries to use solar and wind-fuelled power, rather than electricity, and that demanding they use alternative sources of fuel will further compound their existing poverty.

There was much criticism of the programme. The complaints were investigated by Ofcom (the UK Office of Communications) which reported its findings on 21 July 2008[51]. The Ofcom response to the criticism was that the programme's audience was not materially misled.

---

[51] Ofcom Broadcast Bulletin Issue number 113 – 21/07/08, *www.ofcom.org.uk/tv/obb/prog_cb/obb114/*.

The Danish National Space Center

The Center for Sun-Climate Research at the Danish National Space Center agrees that the climate is changing; however, it does not agree that this change is human-induced or caused by the burning of fossil fuels.

The Danish National Space Center[52] argues that:

'The Earth's climate is always changing. This has been the case in the geological and historical time and even during the last 150 years, where systematic climate measurements have been made, we have seen clear climate changes. Climate changes have both a scientific and a social perspective. The social perspective is associated with the range of climate change that can be attributed to the increasing human induced contribution. The scientific perspective is an endeavour to understand the full complex system of the various sources of climate change and their mutual interactions.
The scientific results indicate that the varying activity of the sun is the largest and most systematic contributor to natural climate variations. Solar activity has been exceptionally high in the 20th century compared to the last 400 years and possibly compared to the past 8,000 years. When solar activity is high, the flux of galactic cosmic rays is reduced due to increased magnetic shielding by the sun. The cosmic rays may influence Earth's climate through formation of low lying clouds.

---

[52] Danish National Space Center, Climate debate and FAQ, *www.spacecenter.dk/research/sun-climate/climate-debate-and-faq/climadebate-and-faq*.

Climate models only include the effects of the small variations in the direct solar radiation (infrared, visible and UV). The effects of cosmic rays on clouds are not included in models and the models do a rather poor job of simulating clouds in the present climate. Since cloud feedbacks are a large source of uncertainty, this is a reason for concern when viewing climate model predictions.'

The Danish National Space Center says that it does not exclude other contributors to rising global temperature. However, it says that there is *'large uncertainty associated with the estimated human contribution'*.

The developing world

There are arguments that the developed and industrialised countries are using the Green Agenda as a trade barrier in order to retain their trade dominance in relation to the developing world.

The economies of the developed world are tightly coupled to energy supply. Reducing the CO_2 levels to the limits suggested by the Kyoto agreement will mean financial costs which in some cases would be severe for the developed countries; this calculation is one of the reasons for the non-signature of countries such as the US.

In addition, the developing countries, not only China, India and Russia but also Africa, need fossil fuels in order to develop. About 30% of the world's population still live without electricity. It is suggested that 'poor countries such as Africa are poor because they are energy poor'[53]. NASA photographs of the Earth at night time show clearly the spread and location of cities; they output enough light to show up as white dots. Such photographs quite clearly show the location of the world's energy users, with the poorer countries showing small clusters of light, and the developed nations showing brighter, larger clusters of light.

Economic growth 'lifts people out of poverty'[54] giving them access to facilities such as electricity and clean water. However, this requires energy as countries develop, particularly in the early stages until the country has sufficient infrastructure to become more energy-efficient.

The BRIC (Brazil, Russia, India and China) countries, in particular India and China, provide benefits for industrialised countries in ways which enable the latter to maintain their hegemony. This has environmental costs, for example, as part of their industrialisation; China is increasing its emissions of CO_2. By 2009, China will be the planet's top emitter of greenhouse gases, according to the International Energy Agency's estimates. Neither China nor India has signed up to the Kyoto agreement. However, there are arguments that environmental trade restrictions in the US and Europe create barriers to trade with the developing countries, because their long-term economic development could threaten the

---

[53] *The Politically Incorrect Guide to Global Warming and Environmentalism*, Christopher Horner, 2007.
[54] *The Mini Rough Guide to Energy and our Planet*, 2008, *www.roughguides.com*.

hegemony of the older, already industrialised nations.

Alarmism

Opponents of the Green Agenda argue that 'the debate around climate change has become highly politicised and alarmist'[55] and that the environmentalist culture is like an authoritarian religion[56].

Simon Jenkins from the *Sunday Times* describes the sense of mass panic and fear-mongering induced by global warming arguments[57]:

'All panics are equal. But some are more equal than others. Present-day government warns us to be very, very afraid, successively of Aids, Saddam Hussein, BSE, terrorists, Sars, bird flu and now global warming. Rulers were once elected to free us from fear, not to increase it. Now they cry wolf every day and use it to demand more power and money into the bargain. Climate change is a hell of a wolf. Last week the BBC's resources were marshalled to produce a royal variety performance of usual suspects: retreating Patagonian glaciers, collapsing Arctic ice shelves,

---

[55] 'Alarmist claims in UN Climate Change Report Refuted', International Policy Network, 7 February 2007, *www.policynetwork.net/main/press_release.php?pr_id=108*.
[56] *The Politically Incorrect Guide to Global Warming and Environmentalism*, Christopher Horner, 2007.
[57] 'Global warming might not be so bad, if we keep our cool', 28 May 2006, Simon Jenkins, *www.timesonline.co.uk/tol/comment/columnists/simon_jenkins/article669171.ece*.

starving Africans, burning rainforests and storm-lashed New Orleans. It was the best of the end of the world, meant to scare us witless.'

One clear example of this alarmist approach is reflected in a photograph that was used by Al Gore, in his film 'An Inconvenient Truth', to provide evidence of global warming. The photograph showed a couple of polar bears standing on top of an iceberg in the open seas. The caption to the photograph reads 'A planet on the edge'. They cling precariously to the top of what is left of the ice flow, their fragile grip the perfect symbol of the tragedy of global warming. Captured on film by Canadian environmentalists the pair of polar bears look stranded on chunks of broken ice

Apparently, however, the photograph was taken two years earlier in August during the Alaskan summer, which is when the ice cap melts each year. The photograph was taken by a student, rather than by Canadian environmentalists and the bears themselves were not far from the coast. In addition, it was pointed out, polar bears are supposed to be good at swimming.

Inadequate temperature and climate records

The scientific hypothesis that the planet is undergoing significant climate change depends fundamentally on the existence of accurate climate measurements over a significant time period, certainly over decades and, ideally, over centuries. It appears that historic methods of measurement are not that accurate.

Dr Stephen Peake is a lecturer in environmental technology at the Open University in the UK. He says that the calculation of mean surface temperature of the earth is measured from three sources[58]:

- Monthly readings from a network of over 3,000 surface temperature observation stations;
- Sea surface temperature measurements; and
- Satellite measurements at lower atmosphere temperatures. These have been available for about the last 30 years.

Measurement of sea surface temperature ranges from 'scooping up a wooden bucket of sea water and sticking a thermometer into it, to measuring the temperature of cooling water entering merchant ships' engine systems'.

Peake says that *'stripping these and other weird and wonderful effects out of the raw historical data throughout the instrumental record has not been trivial. Methods to do this have themselves been the subject of much scientific debate'.*

Over the years, temperature measurement methods have changed and have become more accurate. Temperature records before the mid-nineteenth century are rather small in number and inaccurate. In addition, historical documents tend to describe more extreme events. Peake says: *'as we travel back in time, the uncertainties in our*

---

[58] 'The world around us', Open University, Dr Stephen Peake, *www.open2.net/sciencetechnologynature/worldaroundus /taking_temperature.html*.

measurements of global mean surface temperature cascade'. Some of the less accurate sources include corals, ice cores and tree rings. Peake says that *'There are considerable methodological issues in interpreting data obtained from any of these proxies. Tree ring data, for example, is only available on land while coral data relate only to the tropical and sub tropical regions'.*

The temperature graph used by the IPCC to show global warming indicates that the more recent higher temperatures have been measured on more accurate modern equipment, and have then been compared to the less accurate, older measurements[59]. No firm conclusions would normally be drawn from a comparison of such different measurements.

Special pleading

Many of the organisations that argue that global warming is a man-made problem may have financial incentives to continue promoting this view. The 12 largest environmental pressure groups in the US have a combined annual revenue of $1.95 billion[60]. 'Only 725 of the United States' 20 million companies can boast such magnificent cash flow.'

---

[59] This graph is reproduced on page 35 of *Green IT – Reality, Benefits and Best Practices.*
[60] 'Green Wealth: Funding the Enemy', Alan Caruba, 2006, National Anxiety Center – Greens.

Examples from the report include:

Pressure Group	**Annual revenue**
Nature Conservancy	$731 million
Wildlife Conservation Council	$311 million
The World Wildlife Fund	$118 million
The Sierra Club	$73 million

And so this question may be asked: 'with this revenue to protect, how likely are any of these groups to conclude that global warming is no more than an unproven hypothesis?'

CHAPTER 4: A GREEN IT STRATEGY

Irrespective of one's personal perspective on the green debate, there are a number of good, recognisable commercial reasons for businesses to consider embracing elements of the Green Agenda, particularly in respect of IT activities:

1   Bottom-line benefits: there are significant savings to be achieved from reductions in energy use, and these can directly improve the bottom-line;
2   Protecting or improving the top line: sales may have to be protected and can potentially be increased by applying a green label to products and services;
3   Environmental activism has a role to play in corporate social responsibility agendas;
4   There is a growing range of environmental legal/regulatory requirements[61] to which organisations must conform.

Preston Gralla from Greenbiz sums the situation up well when he says that, in respect of IT:

'There is a very real return on investment associated with Green IT, and it can ultimately be clearly measured. When enterprises go green, they also make green as well, in the form of cash. Virtualisation is good for the environment because it saves electricity, for example. But in doing so, it also saves companies plenty of money.

---

[61] These are covered in more detail in this Guide's companion: *Compliance for Green IT*, *www.itgovernance.co.uk/products/2199*.

That being said, there is plenty of inertia standing in the way of Green IT. It often requires upfront investment, and it certainly requires plenty of planning and time. It sometimes requires a change of corporate culture. And it can also require a restructuring of job responsibilities, such as getting the IT and facilities departments working more closely together[62].

The bottom-line benefits

Although towards the end of 2008 the price of oil fell back sharply from previous records, the long-term prognostication is that the cost of energy will continue rising and is likely to remain high for a while. For example, the *International Herald Tribune* said that: '*global energy demand will grow by 50% over the next two decades ....despite the high world oil prices which are projected to continue over the long term.........
The expected growth in energy demand is especially dramatic in developing countries, led by China, that are expected to have continued strong economic growth over the next two decades*'[63].

These increased fuel prices are due not only to the increased demand for energy and to price increases by OPEC, but are also affected by legislation and by policies such as carbon trading in individual

---

[62] 'Greener IT: Is It More than Hype?', Preston Gralla, 25 August 2008, *www.greenercomputing.com/column/2008/08/25/green-it-is-it-more-hype*.

[63] 'Global energy demand to grow 50%, US agency predicts', 25 June 2008, *www.iht.com/articles/2008/06/25/business/25energy.php*.

countries which are designed to reduce CO_2 emissions[64].

Wide coverage in the IT press of the energy costs of IT equipment and, in particular, of data centres, has placed this issue on the to be addressed list of today's boards. For example, the *New York Times* reports that '*the world's data centers are projected to surpass the airline industry as a greenhouse gas polluter by 2020...... computer servers are used at only six per cent of their capacity on average, while data center facilities as a whole are used at 56% of peak performance*'[65]. According to Gartner[66], ICT has already been blamed for creating two per cent of the world's total CO_2 emissions, which is equivalent to that due to airlines – and this statistic has been widely quoted. Other, equally weighty assertions include:

- The three year cost of powering and cooling servers is currently 1.5 times the cost of purchasing server hardware. Future projections extending out to 2012 show this multiplier increasing to 22 times the cost of the hardware under worst case assumptions and to almost

---

[64] 'Price jolt: Electricity bills going up, up, up', USA today, 20 June 2008. *www.usatoday.com/money/industries/energy/2008-06-15-power-prices-rising_N.htm*.

[65] 'Data centers are becoming big polluters, study finds', 1 May 2008, *http://bits.blogs.nytimes.com/2008/05/01/data-centers-are-becoming-big-polluters-study-finds/*.

[66] 'Managing the company's carbon footprint', Economist Intelligence Unit, *The Economist*, 2008.

three times under even the best-case assumptions[67].

- 70% of Global 1,000 companies will need to significantly change their data centres[68] in the next five years to meet current and future energy needs[69].

It clearly makes practical business sense for any organisations with a high energy cost component to their operations to focus on methods of reducing their energy consumption. Options for doing this include:

- Managing the temperature of the data centre;
- Improving the efficiency of data centre power supplies;
- Virtualisation of server software and consolidation of physical servers; and
- Reducing IT power requirements in the working (office and factory floor) environment.

---

[67] 'Data Center Energy Efficiency and Productivity', Kenneth Brill, 2007, The Uptime Institute *http://uptimeinstitute.org/component/option,com_frontpage/Itemid,1/*.

[68] Alternatively spelt 'data center'.

[69] EPA's Data Center Report Misses an Opportunity, Gartner, 9 August 2007, *www.gartner.com/DisplayDocument?id=511908&ref=g_fromdoc*.

The top line – increasing or protecting sales by using a green label

Michael Peeters[70] says that '*suppliers are being compelled to address their own approach on green topics, to help customers deliver on their own environmental objectives*'. At the moment, the public sector is leading the way in terms of green procurement standards. The European Union (EU) is committed to raising the level of green public procurement by 2010. The UK government has set a goal to be among the EU leaders in sustainable procurement by 2009.

There are reports that there will be increased demand for IT equipment which is branded as green. The NCC reports[71] that customers are increasingly purchasing green products; this, in turn, is '*driving a response from the supply side. Many recent surveys suggest the majority of respondents would buy consumer products from companies that demonstrated their environmentally sensitive credentials*'.

Smart2020[72] reports that '*the carbon generated from materials and manufacture is about one quarter of the overall ICT footprint, the rest coming from its use*'. Those organisations that are concerned about their carbon footprint are therefore likely to prefer purchasing from

---

[70] 'Waste not, want not', Michael Peeters and Helen Keele, *Green Computing*, 24 July 2008.

[71] *Everything's gone green… … or more realistically it needs to*, Ian Jones, NCC.

[72] 'Smart2020: Enabling the low carbon economy in the information age', The Climate Group, Global e-sustainability initiative (GeSI), *www.smart2020.org/*.

companies who manufacture using green materials and processes, rather from those who do not.

The John Lewis Partnership (JLP), in the UK, is a classic example of an organisation that has successfully pursued a Green IT agenda for a combination of hard-nosed commercial and socially responsible reasons. *Green IT in Practice*[73], written by the leader of the JLP Green IT project, describes the organisation's approach and progress.

Corporate social responsibility and reputation

The NCC say that the '*emergence of multiple green groups and initiatives may be the result of collective political, industry, consumer and media exuberance, but they do serve to highlight how seriously the whole issue of energy efficiency is being taken*'[74]. Companies are increasingly under pressure to consider their reputation and corporate social responsibility strategy in the light of the Green Agenda.

Conformance to legal/regulatory requirements[75]

The Kyoto agreement and the Green Agenda are being translated into green regulation and legislation that affects businesses in different ways. This legislation is aimed at reducing the

---

[73] *www.itgovernance.co.uk/products/1907*.

[74] *Everything's gone green… … or more realistically it needs to*, Ian Jones, NCC.

[75] For more detailed guidance, see *Compliance for Green IT*, *www.itgovernance.co.uk/products/2199*.

carbon footprint and energy used in the design, manufacture and disposal of IT equipment. These include the Restriction of the User of Certain Hazardous Substances in Electrical and Electronic Equipment (RoHS) and the Waste Electrical and Electronic Equipment (WEEE) Directive. Some legislation and standards, such as RoHS and ENERGY STAR have been initiated in one country with other versions of the same initiative being adopted in other countries. Other initiatives are more country-restricted. The scope of these regulations is international, because electronic goods are sold internationally.

The Green Office

Any Green IT strategy should tackle power consumption and paper usage in the office/work environment as well as in the data centre. While the most significant savings are made where the bulk of data processing is carried out (i.e. the data centre), savings can also be achieved in terms of workstations and related office IT equipment[76].

---

[76] For more detailed guidance on designing and implementing a Green Office strategy, see *The Green Office* (*www.itgovernance.co.uk/products/2200*).

CHAPTER 5: GREEN SOCIAL RESPONSIBILITY

The Green Agenda is increasingly included in the corporate social responsibility agenda of larger organisations.

The development of corporate social responsibility

Corporate social responsibility (CSR) is not a statutory requirement. However, organisations are under increasing pressure to meet CSR expectations. The pertinent issue for organisations and businesses is therefore to decide on the way in which they define their corporate social responsibility action plans to respond to such pressures.

There is a variety of definitions and understandings of CSR. Some regard it as a current trend, some regard it as a 'do-gooding sideshow'[77]. I've said elsewhere that *'Companies may have many motives, not all of them transparent, in pursuing CSR agendas*[78]. *The Economist* has argued that[79] *'CSR is often misguided, or worse. But in practice few big companies can now afford to ignore it'*. A number

---

[77] 'Corporate Social Responsibility. Just good business', 17 January 2008, <u>Just good business | Economist.com</u>.
[78] 'Corporate Governance: A Practical Guide to the Legal Frameworks and International Codes of Practice.'
[79] 'Corporate Social Responsibility. Just good business', 17 January 2008, <u>Just good business | Economist.com</u>.

of companies (such as John Lewis) use CSR as an integral part of their business[80].

1   Wikipedia[81] describes CSR as:
'A concept whereby organisations consider the interests of society by taking responsibility for the impact of their activities on customers, suppliers, employees, shareholders, communities and other stakeholders, as well as the environment. This obligation is seen to extend beyond the statutory obligation to comply with legislation and sees organisations voluntarily taking further steps to improve the quality of life for employees and their families as well as for the local community and society at large.'

2   The European Commission[82] describes CSR as:
'Companies integrating social and environmental concerns in their business operations and in their interaction with their stakeholders on a voluntary basis.'

---

[80] *Green IT in Practice: How one company is approaching the greening of its IT*, Gary Hird, 2008.
[81] 'Corporate Social Responsibility', *http://en.wikipedia.org/wiki/Corporate_social_responsibility*.
[82] 'Assessing opportunities for ICT to Contribute to Sustainable Development', December 2005, Information Society Technologies, European Commission Information Society and Media.

3   Sir Adrian Cadbury describes CSR as the way
    in which[83]:

*'The governance of companies has to conform,
sooner or later, to public opinion. Corporations
work within a governance framework which is set
first by the law and then by regulations emanating
from the regulatory bodies to which they are
subject. In addition, publicly quoted companies
are subject to their shareholders in general
meeting and all companies to the forces of public
opinion.'*

Each of these definitions shares the idea that
organisations should do more than they are
statutorily required to do in terms of mitigating the
potential social and environmental impacts of their
operations. Environmental concerns and the Green
Agenda should clearly be considered when
organisations turn their attention to CSR. There is
certainly a growing expectation amongst
consumers that organisations will take greater care
on these issues and the success of initiatives like
the anti-fur crusade, responsible off-shore
manufacturing, Fairtrade foodstuffs and eco-
tourism all reflect the strength of consumer feeling
and expectations on these issues.

The early adopters of green initiatives are now into
the later phases of their projects; it should not be
surprising that the early and late majority of
organisations are now expected to follow suit.
Whatever their views on the Green Agenda, few

---

[83] *Corporate Governance. A Practical Guide to the Legal
Frameworks and International Codes of Practice*, Alan
Calder, 2008, *www.itgovernance.co.uk/products/1459*.

organisations will be able to successfully deny the importance of responding to this range of issues.

This changing appreciation of the importance of CSR activities is clearly demonstrated in a recent survey[84] of 1,122 global executives carried out by the Economist Intelligence Unit; it shows that corporate responsibility issues have risen in global executives' priorities – and are expected to become more important.

The growing interest in CSR is also reflected in the UK's Companies Act 2006, which introduced a statutory requirement for public companies to report on social and environmental matters[85]. The United Nations promotes corporate responsibility around the world through a New York based group called the Global Compact[86]. Many universities run corporate social responsibility courses, for example the Nottingham Business School provides MBA, MA and MSC courses in CSR as well as an undergraduate course in Business ethics.

The drivers for the increase in CSR activities include:

1   Consumer concern over climate change and socially responsible operations.
2   The growth of the Internet and Web 2.0 technology has meant that embarrassing news can be captured and broadcast to millions instantly. Companies are therefore having to

---

[84] *www.economist.com/media/pdf/200801116CSRResults.pdf*.

[85] 'Corporate Social Responsibility. Just good business', 17January 2008, <u>Just good business | Economist.com</u>.

[86] *www.unglobalcompact.org*.

try harder to protect their reputation and the environment in which they do business.

3   Companies in the UK and elsewhere are increasingly required to report their non-financial performance as well as their financial results[87].

4   Investors are becoming more interested in CSR issues. '$1 out of every $9 under professional management in America now involves an element of "socially responsible investment"'[88].

5   The adoption of CSR provides a competitive advantage. In 2006 Michael Porter and Mark Kramer from the *Harvard Business Review* published a paper on how, if approached in a strategic way, CSR could become part of a company's competitive advantage.

6   Employees are also looking to their employers to embrace CSR. An undergraduate survey conducted in the UK in 2003[89] found that 80% of respondents said that they would be 'more likely to stay in their jobs if their employer adopted a responsible approach to the work-life balance'.

7   Consumers have a more positive image of companies which adopt a CSR strategy. The UK Nottingham Business School reports that *'over 85% of consumers have a more positive image of companies that are seen to be*

---

[87] 'Corporate Social Responsibility. Just good business', 17January 2008. Just good business | Economist.com.
[88] 'Corporate Social Responsibility. Just good business', 17January 2008. Just good business | Economist.com.
[89] 'Profit with a conscience', Professor Jeremy Moon, Nottingham University Business School, 23 March 2005, Press Room – Nottingham University Business School.

pursuing more responsible business practices and over half of European consumers say they are prepared to pay more for environmentally responsible products. Businesses want to work with other businesses that reflect their own values and attitudes – and those of their customers. If as a business you are behaving in a way which doesn't accord with the way your customers think you should be behaving, it can withdraw your license to operate. Look at Andersen. It was tainted by the actions of its client Enron and disowned by the market[90]. Fairtrade is an example of a business whose growth is entirely dependent on this greater interest in socially responsible business operations; it announced in May 2008 that global sales of Fairtrade products rose by 47% in 2007, with 2.3 billion Euros (1.8 billion pounds) being spent globally on Fairtrade products[91].

CSR and the environment

Environmental responsibility is right at the heart of CSR; any organisation that is serious about its CSR activity must consider its environmental impact, its position in relation to the Green Agenda, and the way in which it will respond to

---

[90] 'Profit with a conscience', Gareth Chadwick, 21 March 2005, *The Independent*, *http://findarticles.com/p/articles/mi_qn4158/is_2005032 1/ai_n13458685/pg_1*.

[91] 'Sales of ethical Fairtrade label rise sharply', 22 May 2008, Reuters UK, *http://uk.reuters.com/article/domesticNews/idUKL22269 67820080522*.

the green expectations of its customers and its stakeholders. While the environmental footprint of each industry – and of each organisation within it – will depend on the exact nature of that industry (an oil company, for instance, has a very different environmental footprint than an e-commerce business), all Western organisations today use information and communications technology and all organisations can and should, therefore, make ICT a part of their CSR strategy.

The following examples describe ways in which organisations have responded to concerns over climate change as part of their CSR policy:

Mr Hiromichi Shinohara, Associate Senior Vice President Executive Director, Information Sharing Laboratory Group, NTT Japan, says that[92] *'NTT's Corporate Social Responsibility charter includes a commitment to reducing its own environmental impact, both in terms of its inputs (e.g. electricity, water, pulp, fuel, gas etc.) and outputs (carbon dioxide and other GHG emissions, equipment for recycling and disposal etc.). It has set environmental targets for 2010'*. NTT is Japan's largest telecommunication services provider.

---

[92] ITU/MIC Kyoto Symposium on ICTs and Climate Change, 15-16 April 2008, Meeting Summary.

Nigel Wilkinson, Health, Safety and Environment Manager for T-Mobile UK, says that T-Mobile UK has implemented a CSR policy that includes[93]:

- Using free air cooling across their network of 13,000 sites, which uses the outside air to cool telecoms equipment cabinets.
- Introducing simple office practices such as switching off PCs at night, switching off lighting and reconfiguring office heating and cooling.
- Switching to 10% renewable and 90% combined heat and power electrical and actual energy reduction initiatives across the company.
- Rolling out automatic meter reading (AMR) across the company. This enables accurate energy readings to be taken on a half hourly basis, so that the company can pay for actual energy usage rather than estimates. This was an investment of over £2 million, with ongoing operational costs of £100,000 per annum. The accurate energy readings provided by the AMRs have enabled T-Mobile to reduce costs by negotiating better energy tariffs, to view the energy profile of all sites and identify any with unusually high energy use and investigate the cause such as faulty air cooling systems or underperforming equipment, test out new energy-efficient technology and get immediate feedback on the level of energy savings. Overall, the installation of the AMR metres

---

[93] 'Back to basics for the cost of corporate social responsibility', *Eco-Executive* Issue 1, *http://publishing.yudu.com/Aafvk/EcoExecutiveIss1/reso urces/87.htm*.

has enabled a saving of seven per cent a year
on energy bills. Energy bills decreased by
£200,000 in 2007. This means that, providing
the operational costs stay constant, there will
be a 20 year payback period.
- Reducing the amount of waste by recycling
  18% of office-generated waste such as plastic,
  paper, cardboard and aluminium cans and
  reduced overall paper consumption by 21%
  across the business.

CHAPTER 6: GREEN IT ACTION PLAN

There are many reasons for an organisation to commit itself to greening its' IT. As with all corporate decisions, the devil will be in the detail and this is certainly the case where IT projects are concerned – particularly those that will have a broad cultural change of the nature that goes with a Green IT project. A Green IT project should, in the first instance, be treated as a business project, one that has a significant business change element to it.

If the organisation is using ISO14001[94] as the specification for its Environmental Management System (EMS), then it should follow the requirements of that standard and ensure that the PDCA (Plan-Do-Check-Act) cycle is applied to the project.

There are a number of key steps that any organisation should take in creating a Green IT action plan[95]:

1   The organisation's environmental aims and objectives should be logically thought through, clearly described and endorsed at the highest possible level (i.e. by the board or other governing body);

---

[94] *www.itgovernance.co.uk/products/1638*.
[95] *The Green IT Implementation Toolkit* (*www.itgovernance.co.uk/products/2201*) contains the most important documents and tools needed to design and implement such an action plan.

2   Someone on the board, as well as a senior
    executive in the organisation, should be
    nominated to be responsible for the
    governance and executive aspects of the Green
    IT strategy;
3   All stakeholders in the organisation should be
    involved;
4   Measure baseline energy use and/or carbon
    footprint at the outset of the project, monitor
    subsequent changes and establish realistic
    metrics;
5   Formalise and communicate Green IT
    practices and progress to everyone involved.

Set aims and objectives

The Green IT action plan should be clear on the
drivers for the action plan, whether this is to
reduce costs, improve the brand image, add value
to stakeholders/shareholders or provide a
competitive edge. It should, from the outset,
clearly identify where its most significant
environmental impacts are and derive from that
analysis the list of key actions that it will take to
reduce its environmental impact as part of its
overall business strategy. The Green IT action plan
should also be contextualised for the
organisation's corporate social responsibility
agenda – if it has one.

The board, or other governing body, should debate
and support the organisation's environmental
objectives, which should ideally be contained
within an organisation-wide policy statement that
sets out clearly what the organisation aims to do,
why, and how its environmental strategy will be
implemented.

The Green IT action plan should look not only at what the IT organisation is doing internally, but also at ways in which IT can be used to save energy and reduce costs in other areas of the organisation. IBM says that the Green IT action plan needs to consider IT and site/facilities together[96].

Nominate someone in the organisation to be responsible for Green IT

The Green IT action plan, once adopted by the board, should continue to receive board oversight through at least one board member, who will ensure that appropriate board support is provided where necessary, and who will also keep fellow board members informed as to implementation progress.

There should also be a senior executive who is responsible for Green IT. As with all change projects, the more senior the executive who is charged with leading the project, the more seriously the organisation will take the project. Moreover, more senior executives are more able to deploy the resources required by the project and iron out the conflicts that might interfere with its completion. This role could be strongly tied in

---

[96] Derived from 'The Green Data Center: Steps for the Journey', IBM Redpaper, August 2008, *www.redbooks.ibm.com/abstracts/redp4413.html*.

with a CSR role. IBM suggests having a dedicated team who are responsible for Green IT[97].

The senior executive who is responsible for Green IT should be the project director, cheerleader and missionary for the Green IT project; this person should certainly be of sufficient seniority to deliver the resources and active commitment of the organisation to the green initiative.

Involve all stakeholders

Implementing Green IT will, in one way or another, affect everyone in the organisation; it is an organisation-wide issue and not one that is just limited to the IT operation. All stakeholders throughout the business therefore need to be involved if the Green IT action plan is to succeed. In many organisations, there is still a sense that the energy efficiency of IT equipment is solely the domain of the IT department – whereas our view is that the Green IT action plan needs to be something which is embraced by the entire organisation, so that the users of energy take responsibility for its costs. A recent survey by the NCC[98] reports that *'IT directors tend to take responsibility for Green IT, rather than a sustainability director or somebody outside IT. Firms are trusting their IT guys to come up with*

---

[97] Derived from 'The Green Data Center: Steps for the Journey', IBM Redpaper, August 2008, *www.redbooks.ibm.com/abstracts/redp4413.html*.

[98] 'Knowledge gap in green IT is hampering further adoption', *Computing*, 28 August 2008, *www.computing.co.uk/computing/news/2224768/knowledge-gap-green-hampering-4196683*.

environmental directives'. For most organisations, this will prove ineffective – the folk that use IT equipment need to buy in to changes that affect its use, otherwise they will find workarounds for those changes which may ultimately undermine achievement of the plan's objectives.

Measure the baseline energy use levels – establish metrics

What gets measured, gets done. This basic truth of management applies as much to Green IT as to anything else.

A recent survey by the NCC[99] suggests that *'many firms are still not evaluating their IT carbon footprint before deciding the best way to start reducing it'*. Having set some headline objectives in the Green IT action plan, the starting point from which progress is to be measured, and the metrics that will be used to monitor effectiveness, needs to be established.

One of the difficulties with measurably reducing energy consumption in data centres has been that reliable figures for energy use have been hard to obtain. In addition, the team within an organisation responsible for paying the energy bills is often not the same as the team responsible for reducing energy requirements. James Murray of *IT Week* says of business concerns about energy consumption that *'the key business argument that it delivers financial savings often lacks impact*

---

[99] 'Knowledge gap in green IT is hampering further adoption', *Computing*, 28 August 2008, *www.computing.co.uk/computing/news/2224768/knowled ge-gap-green-hampering-4196683*.

because the IT department never even sees its electricity bills... Currently, many IT purchasing decisions are made as if buying a car knowing that someone else has promised to pay for the petrol. A few eco-warriors may go for efficiency, but the vast majority will buy the most powerful model they can, regardless of running costs[100].

The Green Grid defines a metric as *'a measuring stick...........A metric is a scale for measuring some important characteristic of an object or system and includes a procedure or methodology for making this measurement. Implementing a metric allows the manager of a system to know how well the system is performing at some point in time. This makes it possible to adjust one or more tunable parameters of the system and assess the impact on the system when measured again utilising the same metric. In this way it becomes possible to optimise whatever aspect of the system that the metric quantifies. To obtain a specific desired goal for the system, however, the particular metric one utilises must be chosen carefully*[101].

---

[100] 'Watch your data centre grow greener (minimise the electricity consumption)', James Murray, *IT Week* (UK), 12 March 2007.
[101] 'A Framework for Data Center Energy Productivity', The Green Grid 2008, *www.thegreengrid.org/sitecore/content/Global/Content/ white-papers/Framework-for-Data-Center-Energy-Productivity.aspx*.

Bruce Nordman from the Lawrence Berkeley National Laboratory[102] says that benchmarks need to be reliable, portable, scaleable and simple. The key requirements are '*Linearity (proportional increases in performance result in the same proportional increase in the metric), Reliability (performance ranking by the metric should directly correspond to ranking of performance in general), Repeatability, Ease of Measurement (so that it will be used, and used correctly), Consistency (of application to different systems), and Independence (of parties biased towards a particular manufacturer)*'.

While the theory is clear, the practice is more difficult. Most performance metrics for IT data centres relate to their efficiency. Comparing metrics for data centres between organisations is not straightforward and is still in its infancy. There is currently a dearth of available data and, in addition, there is not yet a consensus on which metrics should be used. There is also continued disagreement about terminology.

However, despite this, it is essential that organisations carry out some sort of measurement of power usage which can be used as a benchmark against which efficiency improvements can be monitored and measured. One of the organisations which has and is doing much work on this is the Green Grid.

---

[102] 'Metrics of IT Equipment – Computing and Energy Performance', 10 March 2005, *http://hightech.lbl.gov/documents/DATA_CENTERS/Self_benchmarking_guide-2.pdf*.

Formalise and communicate Green IT standards.

Having set the objectives for Green IT and developed a set of processes for meeting the green objectives, these will need to be communicated to everyone involved – both at the outset of the project and on a regular basis thereafter.

The essential point is that implementing a Green IT strategy is essentially a business change project; the same communication challenges, barriers and opportunities as apply to any change project will apply here. A communications plan (involve the corporate communications and/or marketing folk in putting this together) should be drawn up for the Green IT project in the early stages, and should deal with achieving stakeholder buy-in as an early objective.

There should be a clear link between the communications plan and the training activity; those who have a role to play in the Green IT environment may need specific training, and this training should be planned for at an early point. The communication plan can then build in those training events as way points – either for individuals or for the organisation – on the journey towards a better understanding of, and effectiveness with, Green IT.

Once the project has kicked off, communication with stakeholders and those in the business should be on a regular basis and should include regular progress reports – and progress reports should be honest about delays, where these have occurred, and about actions taken to recover a project timeline.

CHAPTER 7: TOP TEN AREAS FOR GREEN IT

Green IT has a significant contribution to make to reduce the organisation's overall cost base. Here are our top ten recommendations (some of which, inevitably, will require some investment in order to implement).

1   Deploy virtualisation software in the data centre and consolidate server hardware and software. Virtualisation and consolidation should then become part of the ongoing IT systems strategy. Make sure that, when you dispose of the now redundant server hardware, you take appropriate steps to protect any confidential information on their hard disks, and you track disposal in line with WEEE regulations.

2   Review your arrangements for data centre cooling; allow a larger range of temperatures and re-configure your airflows to limit power requirements[103].

3   Introduce simple office practices such as switching off PCs at night, switching off lighting and reconfiguring office heating and cooling. You could call this power management and deploy a technology solution to support and control the strategy.

4   Introduce video-conferencing: where possible, have meetings take place across the Internet using third party video-conferencing technology. If necessary, fall back to

---

[103] See the highly informative and helpful *Greening the Data Center*, by George Spafford (ITGP, 2009).

teleconferencing, which is capable of providing a significant reduction in costs without an equal reduction in communicativeness. There are skills to tech-conferencing, but they are easily learned.

5   Increase telecommuting: more staff may be able to work from home than you think. Yes, it may require a bit of effort in terms of planning, equipping and managing, but it can produce significant office cost savings, improve productivity and decrease the organisation's carbon footprint by reducing employee miles.

6   Reduce paper consumption: again, it may take a bit of effort to shift to electronic documentation and archiving, but the savings in paper consumption and paper storage costs – and improvements in productivity – can be significant.

7   Recycle office waste: it is very simple to deploy recycling stations (through an appropriate subcontract) right through an office and to encourage staff to recycle all paper, packaging and so on. Make sure that you have appropriate provision, where necessary, for shredding and secure recycling, to take care of confidential information and information that might be used in identity crimes.

8   Review your equipment lifecycle: ensure that procurement and disposal arrangements for IT equipment take green criteria into account where these are commercially sensible and avoid the negative publicity that can accrue to organisations that don't care!

9   Consider Cloud Computing: this is the increasingly fashionable name for what we've only just got to know as Software as a Service (SaaS), by which software applications are made available across the Internet by a third party (e.g. Salesforce.com) thereby reducing the need for individual organisations to invest in their own hardware and software (plus IT staff) to run similar services.

10   Measure: sooner or later, you'll want to know what progress you're making on a Green IT implementation plan, so ensure that you measure the baseline (i.e. what your performance looks like before you apply green measures) and then at regular points thereafter. In particular, concentrate on measuring the reductions in energy consumed and consequent bottom-line cost savings.

APPENDIX: GREEN GLOSSARY

* Terms taken from the definitions in Alan Calder and Steve Watkins, *A Dictionary of Information Security Terms, Abbreviations and Acronyms* (IT Governance Publishing, 2007).

Air handling unit (AHU) – This cools or heats outside air depending on the ambient temperature and the required internal air temperature[104].

Annex 1 country – A country which has a Kyoto obligation to reduce their CO_2 emissions.

Anthropogenic – 'Made by people or resulting from human activities. Usually used in the context of emissions that are produced as a result of human activities'[105].

Benchmark – 'To evaluate by comparison to a standard. In the context of energy efficiency, benchmarking involves measuring the energy performance of a product or building by means of a standard metric, e.g. kWh of annual energy use per square foot of building floor area. The measured performance value can then be compared to the performance of similar products or buildings'[106].

---

[104] 'The Green Data Center: Steps for the Journey', August 2008, *www.redbooks.ibm.com/abstracts/redp4413.html*.

[105] Glossary, Earth Observatory, *http://earthobservatory.nasa.gov/Library/glossary.php3?mode=all*.

[106] 'EPA Report to Congress on Server and Data Center Energy Efficiency. Appendices.'

Blade server – `A blade server is a server chassis housing multiple thin, modular electronic circuit boards, known as server blades. Each blade is a server in its own right, often dedicated to a single application. The blades are literally servers on a card, containing processors, memory, integrated network controllers, an optional fiber channel host bus adaptor (HBA) and other input/output (IO) ports.

Blade servers allow more processing power in less rack space, simplifying cabling and reducing power consumption. According to a SearchWinSystems.com article on server technology, enterprises moving to blade servers can experience as much as an 85% reduction in cabling for blade installations over conventional 1U or tower servers. With so much less cabling, IT administrators can spend less time managing the infrastructure and more time ensuring high availability.

Each blade typically comes with one or two local ATA or SCSI drives. For additional storage, blade servers can connect to a storage pool facilitated by a network-attached storage (NAS), Fiber Channel, or SCSI storage-area network (SAN). The advantage of blade servers comes not only from the consolidation benefits of housing several servers in a single chassis, but also from the consolidation of associated resources (like storage and networking equipment) into a smaller architecture that can be managed through a single interface.

A blade server is sometimes referred to as a high-density server and is typically used in a cluster of servers that are dedicated to a single task, such as:

- File sharing;
- Web page serving and caching;
- SSL encrypting of Web communication;
- The transcoding of web page content for smaller displays;
- Streaming audio and video content.

Like most clustering applications, blade servers can also be managed to include load balancing and failover capabilities'[107]

Cap-and-trade system – Under a cap-and-trade system, a mandatory cap or minimum carbon emissions reduction target to be achieved is set. The cap-and-trade system usually applies to countries, regions or larger organisations. The cap is set by regulation and/or taxes, or in the case of countries and regions, by political negotiation.

Carbon credit – Each carbon credit is equal to the reduction of one tonne of CO_2 emissions.

Certified Emission Reductions (CER) – are units of greenhouse gas reductions generated from CDM projects. They are verified by external, UN-accredited third party verifiers, and issued by the regulatory body of CDM, the CDM Executive Board. CERs can be used for compliance with Kyoto Protocol obligations or to meet emissions caps under the European Union Emissions Trading

---

[107] 'What is a blade server?' SearchDataCenter.com. *http://searchdatacenter.techtarget.com/sDefinition/0,,sid80_gci770169,00.html.*

Scheme. CERs should be distinguished from VERs, which are used in a voluntary trading scheme.

Chiller – This is used to remove heat from a data centre[108]. The term is sometimes used to describe the device that chills water that is used as the transfer medium for heat removal.

Climate change – The IPCC[109] refer to climate change as 'any change in climate over time, whether due to natural variability or as a result of human activity'. This differs from the definition of climate change from the United Nations Framework Convention on Climate Change (UNFCCC), where climate change refers to a change of climate that is attributed directly or indirectly to humans. The term climate change is used synonymously with global warming by some environmentalists, but this concept is different.

Computer server – This is defined by ENERGY STAR[110] as 'A computer that provides services and manages networked resources for client129 devices, e.g., desktop computers, notebook computers, thin clients, wireless devices, PDAs, IP130 telephones, other computer servers and other networked devices'.

---

[108] 'The Green Data Center: Steps for the Journey', August 2008,
www.redbooks.ibm.com/abstracts/redp4413.html.
[109] 'Climate Change 2007: Synthesis Report', IPCC,
www.ipcc.ch/ipccreports/ar4-syr.htm.
[110] 'ENERGY STAR Program Requirements for Computer Servers Draft', 2 July 2008,
www.energystar.gov/index.cfm?c=new_specs.enterprise _servers.

CPU* – The central processing unit.

Data – A collection of facts from which conclusions may be drawn[111].

DC Server – This is defined by ENERGY STAR[112] as 'A computer server designed to operate with a DC-DC power supply or 157 a server which runs directly off DC voltage supplied to internal DC-DC converters from an external 158 source'.

Direct methanol fuel cell – 'Electrochemical alternative energy device that converts high-energy density fuel (liquid methanol) directly to electricity'[113].

Double counting – This term is used within the context of carbon trading to refer to a carbon offset being sold more than once. The carbon offset should only be sold once. Once the offset is used, it needs to be retired to ensure that the benefit of the reductions is only counted once. A failure to do this is called double counting.

Economiser – A mechanical device intended to reduce energy consumption in buildings[114]. Economisers make use of outside air, or water as a

---

[111] WordNet,
http://wordnet.princeton.edu/perl/webwn?s=data.
[112] 'ENERGY STAR Program Requirements for Computer Servers Draft', 2 July 2008,
www.energystar.gov/index.cfm?c=new_specs.enterprise_servers.
[113] 'SMART 2020: Enabling the low carbon economy in the information age', The Climate Group 2008.
[114] 'Economizer', Wikipedia,
http://en.wikipedia.org/wiki/Economizer.

means of cooling the indoor space within a data centre.

Electrostatic – Pertaining to static electricity[115].

Energy efficiency – Rasmussen defines energy efficiency as follows: 'The more energy-efficient a system is, the more workload it can process with a certain power input'[116].

Equipment failure – Pinheiro et al have reported on the difficulties in consistently defining failure across organisations with respect to disk drives[117]. Generally, we are defining failure here as anything which causes downtime, that is, which causes the equipment or software not to work. Pinheiro et al refer to the Annual Failure Rate (AFR), or refer to the Mean Time Between Failure (MTBF)[118]. Failure can be caused by temperature (too hot or too cold), shock, vibration, and power quality.

Extended producer responsibility – This is an aspect of waste disposal legislation, whereby producers and manufacturers are responsible for 'financing and organising take-back and recycling

---

[115] 'EPA Report to Congress on Server and Data Center Energy Efficiency. Appendices.'

[116] 'Electrical Efficiency Modeling for Data Centers', Rasmussen, 2007, American Power Conversion. *www.apcmedia.com/salestools/NRAN-66CK3D_R1_EN.pdf*.

[117] 'Failure Trends in a Large Disk Drive Population', Pinheiro et al, February 2007. Taken from the Proceedings of the 5th USENIX Conference on file and Storage Technologies (FAST '07).

[118] 'Thinking inside the box: Boosting the effectiveness of air cooling', May 2008, David Lippincott, Chassis Plans, *www.mil-embedded.com/articles/id/?3281*.

of waste batteries, packaging, end-of-life vehicles (ELVs), and waste electrical and electronic equipment (WEEE)'[119].

Fuel cell – A fuel cell is an electrochemical device that converts chemical energy directly into electrical energy[120].

GHG – Green House Gas.

Global warming – Global warming is defined by Wikipedia[121] as the increase in the average measured temperature of the Earth's near-surface air and oceans since the mid-twentieth century, and its projected continuation.

Gray water – Waste water from all fixtures except toilets[122].

Green collar – The description (as in blue collar, white collar, etc.) applied to those who have manual labour jobs in the new, green economy. No one is yet sure how a sustainable green economy will be able to continue generating increases in

---

[119] 'Strategic, Financial, and Design Implications of Extended Producer Responsibility in Europe: A Producer Case Study', Greener Computing, 1 January 2008. *www.greenercomputing.com/resources/resource/strategi c-financial-and-design-implications-extended-producer-responsibility-euro*.

[120] 'Fuel Cell Systems: Efficient, Flexible Energy Conversion for the 21st Century', Elliss et al, 2001, Proceedings of the IEEE, Vol. 89, No. 12 December 2001.

[121] 'Global warming', Wikipedia, *http://en.wikipedia.org/wiki/Global_warming*.

[122] 'Kitchen, Bath and Plumbing Words Dictionary', PlumbingWorld.com, *www.plumbingworld.com/plumbingdefinitions.html*.

employment opportunities in the way that the old, unsustainable one did, but that's a subject for another book.

The Greenhouse effect – This is the increase in climate temperature caused by increases in CO_2[123]. The Earth is surrounded by an atmosphere which protects it from harmful solar radiation and supports all living things. It is made of air which is a mixture of oxygen (21%), nitrogen (78%), carbon dioxide (0.037%) and other gases such as hydrogen, helium, argon, neon, krypton, xenon and ozone. The atmosphere is more permeable to incoming solar radiation than outgoing infrared radiation and therefore traps heat. If this were not the case, the Earth would be too cold for us to survive. It is the artificial or man-made increase of the concentration of carbon dioxide in this atmosphere which leads to significant changes in surface temperatures.

Greenwashing – This term is widely used to describe the inappropriate use of green concepts in order to present an artificially positive image of a company. The term is often used in a derogatory way, particularly towards large, profit-conscious corporate organisations. Definitions include:

1   The Free Dictionary – 'The dissemination of misleading information by an organisation to conceal its abuse of the environment in order to present a positive public image'[124].

---

[123] 'Stern Review on the economics of climate change', HM Treasury, UK, 2005, www.occ.gov.uk/activities/stern.htm.
[124] The free dictionary, Greenwash, www.thefreedictionary.com/greenwash.

2 Concise Oxford Dictionary – 'Disinformation disseminated by an organisation so as to present an environmentally responsible public image'[125].

3 Corpwatch – 'The phenomenon of socially and environmentally destructive corporations attempting to preserve and expand their markets by posing as friends of the environment and leaders in the struggle to eradicate poverty'[126].

We do not believe that adopting a commercially pragmatic Green IT strategy could be defined as greenwashing; even if it were, the business benefits will still be worth having. Companies who want to avoid being branded as greenwashers may sometimes keep 'their green initiatives largely to themselves, enjoying the other business benefits these efforts bring – reduced costs, decreased risks, improved quality, increased employee satisfaction, etc. – but foregoing the reputational benefits'[127].

HDD – Hard disk drive.

Hegemony – this refers to the situation in which one country or group of countries or social group is the strongest and most powerful and therefore able to control or dominate others. Examples of (potentially) hegemonic states in history are the

---

[125] Concise Oxford English Dictionary, 10th edition.
[126] Defining Greenwash, CorpWatch, *www.corpwatch.org/article.php?id=943*.
[127] 'How Bad is Greenwashing, Really?', GreenerComputing, *www.greenercomputing.com/column/2008/07/06/how-bad-is-greenwashing-really*.

Roman Empire, the British Empire, the United States and the united Germany that had existed from 1871 to 1945[128].

High-end servers – Defined by market research firm IDC as servers with an average sales value of $500,000 or more[129].

Homeostasis – The property of a living organism to maintain a stable, constant condition[130]. Wikipedia defines homeostasis as the property of a living organism that regulates its internal environment so as to maintain a stable, constant condition[131].

HVAC – Heating, Ventilation and Air Conditioning.

Hygroscopic – Tending to absorb moisture[132].

Infrastructure equipment – All equipment in a building outside of the IT equipment racks, such as the HVAC system, PDUs, UPSs, and building lighting[133].

---

[128] 'Hegemony', Wikipedia, *http://en.wikipedia.org/wiki/Hegemony*.

[129] 'EPA Report to Congress on Server and Data Center Energy Efficiency. Appendices.'

[130] 'Homeostasis', Wikipedia, *http://en.wikipedia.org/wiki/Homeostasis*.

[131] 'Homeostasis', Wikipedia, *http://en.wikipedia.org/wiki/Homeostasis*.

[132] 'Plastic Containers Glossary', All-Pak stock products, *www.all-pak.com/plasticgloss.asp?navid=42#h*.

[133] 'EPA Report to Congress on Server and Data Center Energy Efficiency. Appendices.'

Integrated Product Policy – The European Commission defines the Integrated Product Policy as:

'All products cause environmental degradation in some way, whether from their manufacturing, use or disposal. Integrated Product Policy (IPP) seeks to minimise these by looking at all phases of a product's life-cycle and taking action where it is most effective.

The life-cycle of a product is often long and complicated. It covers all the areas from the extraction of natural resources, through their design, manufacture, assembly, marketing, distribution, sale and use to their eventual disposal as waste. At the same time it also involves many different factors such as designers, industry, marketing people, retailers and consumers. IPP attempts to stimulate each part of these individual phases to improve their environmental performance.

With so many different products and actors there cannot be one simple policy measure for everything. Instead there is a whole variety of tools – both voluntary and mandatory – that can be used to achieve this objective. These include measures such as economic instruments, substance bans, voluntary agreements, environmental labelling and product design guidelines'[134].

---

[134] 'What is Integrated Produce Policy?', European Commission, *http://ec.europa.eu/environment/ipp/integratedpp.htm*.

ISO14001 – This standard specifies the requirements for an environmental management standard[135].

LEED certification – The 'Leadership in Energy and Environmental Design (LEED) Green Building Rating System™ encourages and accelerates global adoption of sustainable green building and development practices through the creation and implementation of universally understood and accepted tools and performance criteria'[136].

Microprocessor – Wikipedia says that the 'microprocessor incorporates most or all of the functions of a central processing unit (CPU) on a single integrated circuit (IC)'[137].

Mid-range servers – Defined by market research firm IDC as servers with an average sales value of $25,000 to $499,999[138].

MOT – Ministry of Transport. The MOT Test certificate provides proof that a vehicle is properly maintained and that it complies with certain legal requirements.

Mtoe – Million Tonne of Oil Equivalent. This is the amount of oil required to release the same

---

[135] 'ISO14001', Environmental Management, *www.iso14000-iso14001-environmental-management.com/iso14001.htm*.

[136] 'LEED Rating Systems', US Green Building Council, *www.usgbc.org/DisplayPage.aspx?CMSPageID=222*.

[137] 'Microprocessor', Wikipedia, *http://en.wikipedia.org/wiki/Microprocessor*.

[138] 'EPA Report to Congress on Server and Data Center Energy Efficiency. Appendices.'

amount of energy as another energy source such as coal.

OPEC – The organisation of the Petroleum Exporting Countries (OPEC) consists of 12 nations, Angola, Algeria, Indonesia, Iran, Iraq, Kuwait, Libya, Nigeria, Qatar, Saudi Arabia, the United Arab Emirates and Venezuela. OPEC controls 77% of world crude oil reserves and 43% of its natural gas. The organisation acts as a cartel by agreeing output and oil price targets[139].

Outage – Discontinuance of electricity supply.

PACS – Picture Archiving and Communications System (PACS) enables images such as x-rays and scans to be stored and viewed electronically, thus dramatically reducing the cost and time taken to make patient diagnoses and care[140].

Petrol and Gasoline – Gasoline and petrol are both used to describe the oil or petroleum product used to fuel cars and airplanes. Gasoline is the term used in the United States, petrol is the term used in other English speaking countries.

Power density – Power of a given set of equipment divided by a given area of floor space[141]:

---

[139] *The Mini Rough Guide to Energy and our Planet*, 2008, *www.roughguides.com*.

[140] *www.connectingforhealth.nhs.uk/systemsandservices/ pacs*.

[141] 'EPA Report to Congress on Server and Data Center Energy Efficiency. Appendices.'

- **Computer power density** – Power drawn by the computer equipment divided by the computer room floor area.
- **Building power density** – Total power drawn by the building divided by the total floor area of the building.
- **Total computer room power density** – Power drawn by the computer equipment and all supporting equipment such as PDUs, UPSs, HVAC, and lighting divided by the computer room floor area.

Power Distribution Unit (PDU) – The PDU is a piece of equipment within the data centre which transforms the inputted power to the right phase and voltage and then delivers it to the IT equipment.

Power Supply – This is another name for the PDU. It is defined by ENERGY STAR[142] as 'A self-contained server component which converts a voltage input to one or more different DC voltage output(s) for the purpose of powering the server. The input voltage can be from either an AC or DC source. A computer server power supply must be separable from the main computer board and must connect to the system via a removable or hard-wired male/female electrical connection, cable, cord or other wiring (i.e. separate from and not integrated onto the system motherboard)'.

Pump – This is used in the data centre to circulate water through the data centre via computer room

---

[142] 'ENERGY STAR Program Requirements for Computer Servers Draft', 2 July 2008, www.energystar.gov/index.cfm?c=new_specs.enterprise_servers.

air conditioning (CRAC) units, in-row cooling units, and rear door heat exchangers[143].

Rack – Electronic equipment is often housed in a metal framework called an equipment rack. Usually, an equipment rack contains multiple bays, each designed to hold a unit of equipment such as a computer server. Typically, the equipment unit is mounted (inserted into a bay in the rack) and secured in place with a screw[144].

RCI – Rack cooling index.

REC – Renewable energy certificates. One REC equals the generation of 1,000 kWh of green power by a regional wind farm or other renewable energy source[145].

Redundancy – When used in the context of data storage, the term redundancy describes 'computer or network system components, such as fans, hard disk drives, servers, operating systems, switches, and telecommunication links that are installed to back up primary resources in case they fail. A well-known example of a redundant system is the redundant array of independent disks'[146].

---

[143] The Green Data Center: Steps for the Journey',
August 2008,
www.redbooks.ibm.com/abstracts/redp4413.html.

[144] 'Rack-mounted', whatis.com,
http://whatis.techtarget.com/definition/0,,sid9_gci84792 3,00.html.

[145] '3Degrees Utility Partner, AmerenUE, Makes It Even Easier for Customers to Support Renewable Energy',
www.3degreesinc.com/press/news_article/133/.

[146] SearchStorage.com, Redundant,
http://searchstorage.techtarget.com/sDefinition/0,,sid5_g ci213987,00.html.

Relative humidity – an index of the water content of air, expressed as a percentage of the maximum amount of water the air can hold at that temperature[147].

RoHS – Reduction of hazardous substances.

SAN – Storage Area Network. SearchStorage.com defines this as 'a high speed, special purpose network which interconnects different kinds of data storage devices with associated data servers on behalf of a larger network of users'[148].

SATA (Serial Advanced Technology Attachment) drives – This is a computer bus primarily designed for the transfer of data between a computer and mass storage devices such as hard disk drives and optical drives. The main advantages of SATA over the older parallel ATA interface are faster data transfer, the ability to remove or add devices while operating (hot swapping), thinner cables that let air cooling work more efficiently, and more reliable operation with tighter data integrity checks[149]. A SATA drive can cost anything from £30 to £62 ($53 to $111).

Sequestration – The David Suzuki Foundation describes sequestration sinks as the 'process of increasing the carbon content of a carbon pool other than the atmosphere. Under the Kyoto Protocol, developed countries can meet part of

---

[147] 'EPA Report to Congress on Server and Data Center Energy Efficiency. Appendices'.

[148] 'Storage area network', SearchStorage.com, *http://searchstorage.techtarget.com/sDefinition/0,,sid5_g ci212937,00.html*.

[149] 'Serial ATA', Wikipedia, *http://en.wikipedia.org/wiki/Serial_ATA*.

their emission reduction commitments by enhancing the storage of carbon in the biosphere through certain land use change and forestry activities'[150].

Server* – This is the name given to a computer on a network that stores shared information or which handles common tasks for a number of client computers.

Server consolidation – The consolidation of multiple applications on fewer hardware-based servers[151].

Server farm* (also, server cluster). A collection of networked, load-balanced servers in a single secure site that are capable of accomplishing more than a single server through task distribution. This also helps provide operational redundancy back-up.

Set point – Within the context of data centres, this refers to the baseline average temperature[152].

Software as a service – (SaaS) describes the delivery of a software application as a service via the Web.

Spark spread – The spark spread is the relative difference between the price of fuel and the price of power. Spark spread is highly dependent on the

---

[150] 'Taking Credit', David Suzuki Foundation.
[151] 'EPA Report to Congress on Server and Data Center Energy Efficiency. Appendices.'
[152] 'Data Center Cooling Set Points Debated', 24 September 2007, Data Center Knowledge, *www.datacenterknowledge.com/archives/2007/09/24/dat a-center-cooling-set-points-debated/*.

efficiency of conversion. For a CHP system, spark spread is the difference between the cost of fuel for the CHP system to produce power and heat on site and the offset cost of purchased grid power[153].

SWaP (Space, Watts and Performance) metric – Metric used to evaluate the efficiency of a server within the constraints of space and power consumption[154].

Thin client – This is a comparatively low cost, centrally managed computer which notionally has fewer applications running on it than a PC. A thin client will not have CD-ROM players, diskette drives or expansion slots. A thin client will also therefore require less power and has a longer lifespan.

UPS* – An Uninterruptible Power Supply is a device which is designed to keep other electricity powered devices operating when the normal power supply fails. A UPS should, at the very least, be rated as capable of meeting the power requirements of the device(s) it is supporting for long enough to allow an orderly shutdown of the services. The length of time required for this may need to be ascertained by testing. These also handle a range of other tasks, including smoothing out power fluctuations and power spikes.

---

[153] 'Definitions', Definitions | Combined Heat and Power Partnership Home | US EPA.
[154] 'SWaP (Space, Watts and Performance) Metric', www.sun.com/servers/coolthreads/swap/learnmore.jsp#more.

Utilisation – Pinheiro et al[155] quote the definition of utilisation, when applied to disk drives (and therefore servers) as the 'fraction of time a drive is active out of the total powered-on time'.

Vampire energy – Energy which is used when a device is switched off. Appliances using vampire energy include those with external power supplies, such as inkjet printers, or those with internal clocks and sensors. These also include CPUs, monitors, printers, scanners, fax machines, copiers and water coolers[156].

Verified or Voluntary Emissions Reductions (VERs) – These are reductions which, unlike CERs are sold on the voluntary market. They are not linked to the Kyoto Protocol[157].

Virgin paper – Paper which hasn't been used before.

Volume servers – Defined by market research firm IDC as servers with an average sales value below $25,000[158].

---

[155] 'Failure Trends in a Large Disk Drive Population', Pinheiro et al, February 2007. Taken from the Proceedings of the 5th USENIX Conference on file and Storage Technologies (FAST '07).

[156] 'How to eliminate electricity vampires and save on your bills', *http://financemanila.net/2008/06/11/how-to-eliminate-electricity-vampires-and-save-on-your-bills/*.

[157] 'Making Sense of the Voluntary Carbon Market, A Comparison of Carbon Offset Standards', Kollmuss et al, March 2008, WWF.

[158] 'EPA Report to Congress on Server and Data Center Energy Efficiency. Appendices.'

ITG RESOURCES

IT Governance Ltd source, create and deliver products and services to meet the real-world, evolving IT governance needs of today's organisations, directors, managers and practitioners. The ITG website (*www.itgovernance.co.uk*) is the international one-stop-shop for corporate and IT governance information, advice, guidance, books, tools, training and consultancy.

www.itgovernance.co.uk/green-it.aspx is the ITG website that includes a comprehensive range of books, tools and project templates for Green IT and ISO14001.

Pocket Guides

For full details of the entire range of pocket guides, simply follow the links at *www.itgovernance.co.uk/publishing.aspx*. The current range includes the following companions to this guide:

The Green Office
www.itgovernance.co.uk/products/2200

Compliance for Green IT
www.itgovernance.co.uk/products/2199

The Governance of Green IT
www.itgovernance.co.uk/products/2106

Toolkits

ITG's unique range of toolkits includes the *Green IT Implementation Toolkit*, which contains all the tools and guidance that you will need in order to develop and implement an appropriate Green IT action plan

for your organisation. Full details can be found at
www.itgovernance.co.uk/products/2201.

Best Practice Reports

ITG's new range of Best Practice Reports is now at
www.itgovernance.co.uk/best-practice-reports.aspx.
These offer you essential, pertinent, expertly
researched information on an increasing number of
key issues, including Green IT.

Training and Consultancy

IT Governance also offer training and consultancy
services across the entire spectrum of disciplines
in the information governance arena. Details
of training courses can be accessed
at *www.itgovernance.co.uk/training.aspx* and
descriptions of our consultancy services can be found
at *www.itgovernance.co.uk/consulting.aspx*.

Why not contact us to see how we could help you and
your organisation?

Newsletter

IT governance is one of the hottest topics in business
today, not least because it is also the fastest moving,
so what better way to keep up than by subscribing to
ITG's free monthly newsletter *Sentinel*? It provides
monthly updates and resources across the whole
spectrum of IT governance subject matter, including
risk management, information security, ITIL and IT
service management, project governance, compliance
and so much more. Subscribe for your free copy at:
www.itgovernance.co.uk/newsletter.aspx.